W9-CQG-918

LOOKING FOR CALVIN AND HOBBES

The UNCONVENTIONAL
STORY of BILL WATTERSON
and HIS REVOLUTIONARY
COMIC STRIP

For Indie
Everything would be nothing without you

LOOKING FOR CALVIN AND HOBBES

The UNCONVENTIONAL STORY *of* BILL WATTERSON *and* HIS REVOLUTIONARY COMIC STRIP

By Nevin Martell

continuum

2009

The Continuum International Publishing Group Inc
80 Maiden Lane, New York, NY 10038

The Continuum International Publishing Group Ltd
The Tower Building, 11 York Road, London SE1 7NX

www.continuumbooks.com

A catalog record for this book is available from the Library of
Congress.

ISBN 978 0 82642 984 1

Typeset by Pindar NZ, Auckland, New Zealand
Printed in the United States of America

CONTENTS

There is another world,
but it is in this one.

— Paul Eluard

PROLOGUE

If earth suddenly had to be evacuated and I was limited to grabbing the ten best people to save, Watterson would definitely be in there. There is a point where you stop rating people — you just rate them among the best. Can I say that Mozart is better than the Beatles? I can't. I can just say that they both have gone above the cloud layer and are up there near the sun. They both are on that short list of things that are essential. Watterson is an essential.

— Brad Bird, Academy Award-winning
director of *Ratatouille* and *The Incredibles*

I was a diehard *Calvin and Hobbes* fan from the moment I first stumbled across it in the *Utica Observer Dispatch* in 1987. Its creator, Bill Watterson, had been drawing the strip for two years before I discovered it. During that time, he had hit his artistic and story-telling stride, resulting in a *Calvin and Hobbes* that was instantly thought-provoking, eye-catching and funny in a way I had never seen before in the comics section. I loved the relationship between the boy, Calvin, and his pet tiger, Hobbes, which was at turns playful, combative, philosophical and fantastical. They acted and sounded like real best friends. You could feel the depth of caring and understanding between them, although their friendship was constrained within three or four black-and-white panels. In my mind, it was the perfect strip. Calvin and Hobbes did everything that I always wanted to do — they time traveled, dug for dinosaur bones in the backyard and built legions of abominable snowmen. And they always had each other, which made all those adventures even more fun and exciting. Every day, I would cut out the strip and paste it into a black composition notebook, now lost somewhere in my mother's attic, waiting for my future children to discover it. That was my way of joining in and enjoying their fun.

I loved that I could relate to Calvin like no other comic character. Charlie Brown was always too depressed, Garfield was too obsessive-compulsive and Hägar the Horrible was never violent and bloodthirsty enough. On the other hand, Calvin had a wildly creative mind, a devil's flair for mischief and a flamethrower-powered desire to go on as many adventures as possible before his mother made him go to bed. And with Hobbes by his side, Calvin always had someone to play with, talk to and comfort him.

Sometimes Watterson would sketch out memorable parables that drove their point home with a chuckle (often at Calvin's unwitting expense) and at other times he gave us straight-up gags, explored family dynamics or sent his intrepid duo hurtling through time and space and over cliffs. At other times, Watterson made us scramble for the encyclopedia and the dictionary to answer perplexing questions such as, What does Weltanschauung mean?, Is that really what a pteranodon looks like?, and Who are the Australopithecus Woman and Paul Gauguin? But what he always did best was inspire his readers to use their imagination. He wanted you to think about what happened in the slender white spaces between the frames of the strip and beyond its ending. No matter what magic Watterson concocted, there was rarely a moment when the strip felt forced or, worse yet, meaningless.

The true measure of art intended for children is whether it resonates on a deeper level when you interpret it as an adult. J. R. R. Tolkien's books, Walt Disney's movies and the soundtrack to *Yellow Submarine* all took on a new life when I crossed the threshold from youth into relative maturity, and so did *Calvin and Hobbes*. I still learn new things about the work and about myself when I burrow into my old paperback collections on those rare, truly lazy Sundays.

Rivaled only by *Garfield* and *Peanuts*, *Calvin and Hobbes* was one of the most popular comic strips in the world when Watterson suddenly retired it on New Year's Eve, 1995. His departure — as well as that of Gary Larson's *The Far Side* and Berke Breathed's *Outland* that same year — signaled the end of the last Golden Age of newspaper comics. Though there have been some worthy successors to take their places, newspaper comics have failed to collectively seize the zeitgeist and capture the public's imagination in the same way.

Calvin and Hobbes remains incredibly popular today, in spite of a marked lack of promotion. In 2009, Calvin took home the Best Hair in Comics trophy at the first annual Nickelodeon Magazine Comics Awards. When *Opus* retired in late 2008, the *Washington Post*'s *Comic Riffs* blog ran an unofficial poll to ask readers what they'd like to see as a replacement, over 600 fans asked for the paper to rerun *Calvin and Hobbes* strips rather than any new strips. To this day, the collections sell more than a million copies a year around the world. As if to illustrate this point, when I went to Oaxaca,

Mexico, the main bookseller in town told me he couldn't keep the Spanish-language versions on the shelves because they always sold out quickly.

Looking back at *Calvin and Hobbes* now, I would, without hyperbole or doubt, say that Bill Watterson is the most brilliant pop artist of the late twentieth century. Like the masters of cartooning, humor and social commentary who came before him, Watterson stood on the shoulders of giants before becoming one himself. His expansive color Sunday strips and thoughtfully etched black-and-white dailies rivaled the classic cartooning work of his heroes, Charles Schulz, Walt Kelly and George Herriman, while the wonderfully bizarre wars Calvin and Hobbes waged on each other recalled the antics of *MAD* magazine's *Spy Vs. Spy* and their thoughtful discussions were sometimes evocative of *Winnie the Pooh*.

Though Watterson's influences are somewhat easy to ascertain, the man himself is an enigma. During the ten years that *Calvin and Hobbes* was drawn and was entrancing millions and millions of readers around the world, the man behind it tried to remain as anonymous as possible. As the boy and his tiger reached new highs in readership, their creator shrank deeper into self-imposed obscurity. Watterson never felt comfortable sharing himself with his readers in a public way and he never allowed his work to be licensed. On the extremely rare occasion that he did make a public appearance or grant an interview, he only spoke openly about his work and went to great lengths to avoid discussing, or divulging any details from, his personal life.

To call him the J. D. Salinger of American cartooning is to take the easy road, but the fact remains that this incredibly talented comic artist is one of the most elusive characters of the late twentieth century — so elusive, in fact, that only a handful of pictures of him have ever been published. He gave his last interview with a journalist in 1989 and his last public appearance was a commencement speech he gave at his alma mater, Kenyon College, in 1990. Since officially retiring *Calvin and Hobbes*, Watterson has emerged infrequently and sporadically, and never in person.

So how do you find the man who doesn't want to be found? How would that same man react to the idea of a book that sought to examine him at length and in depth? What would I say to Watterson if I got a chance to meet him? What began as a childhood dream turned into a journey through the strata of popular culture to discuss the genius of *Calvin and Hobbes* and Watterson's profound influence.

Initially, I told my friends about the project with equal amounts of boastfulness and fear. I was happy, because this was the gig of a lifetime, but I was afraid of what my peers would make of my work. Because while they said, "Of course I know who Bill Watterson is! *Calvin and Hobbes* was the best comic strip *ever!*" I could read between the lines. What they were really saying was, "If you screw this book up, you will be pissing on some of the fondest memories of my youth. Don't *&@I#? with my inner child . . . I will *not* be amused!" Ultimately, discussion of writing this book was banned from my cocktail-party conversational repertoire in a bid to maintain my sanity.

Frankly, I would have had the same reaction my friends did. I made peace with my inner geek long ago and he has high standards. As a kid, I loved graphic novels, comics strips and comic books, but always fell for the off-the-beaten-track stuff that challenged my imagination: Asterix and Obelix, Tintin, *Groo the Wanderer* and

Elfquest. Okay, so I also loved *G. I. Joe*, *The Punisher* and — before I knew what the word "lame" meant — *The California Raisins*, but none of those mean as much to me in hindsight or resonate as strongly when I reread them now. *Calvin and Hobbes* is different. It's as timeless as Bach's cantatas, *The Count of Monte Cristo* and Reese's Peanut Butter Cups. And that's what everyone I discussed this project with seemed to realize as well.

I am not the first writer to attempt to find Bill Watterson. The *Cleveland Plain Dealer* sent a reporter in 1998 and the *Cleveland Scene* sent out another in 2003 — both men returned empty handed. A bigger expedition was launched by Gene Weingarten, humor columnist for the *Washington Post*, around 2003. Backed by the paper's expense account, his editor's blessing and a first edition of a *Barnaby* book to woo Watterson into cooperating, Weingarten headed to Chagrin Falls, where Watterson was living at the time. Deciding that the best tack would be to approach Watterson's parents, he showed up on their doorstep with a letter to Bill and the book. The letter said Weingarten would be in a nearby hotel room and that he was willing to stay as long as it took for Watterson to contact him. Though he says the Wattersons were kind and promised to pass along his package, they also told him he had no chance of scoring the interview. Nonetheless, he drove to his motel and began his vigil.

The next morning his phone rang. It was Watterson's editor, Lee Salem, telling him to pack his bags and go home, because it was not gonna happen — no where, no how, no Watterson. Weingarten never published an article chronicling this mini-odyssey, but when he told me the story, he did it with a good sense of humor and his best wishes for my success. After I heard Weingarten's account, I didn't know how to feel. On the one hand, I was buoyed by the thought that I might be the first writer to crack into Watterson's inner sanctum in almost two decades. However, it was depressing to know that the path ahead would be littered with the failures of reputable journalists who had given it their all, but to no avail.

On 7 July 2008, about six months into the actual writing of this book, I finally worked up the courage to send a letter to Bill Watterson, in the hope of scoring an interview with him. I had obtained his current address from public records, and thought that a letter would be the least intrusive way of contacting him. After all, showing up on his lawn — like Lloyd Dobbler with his boombox in *Say Anything* — was probably not going to win me any points, and could very well land me in jail. Admittedly, a phone call would have been more direct than a letter, but again, I felt as if Watterson wouldn't appreciate such an intimate intrusion. While the call would be expedient, I was fairly certain that it would hurt my chances.

So, I settled down and wrote him a letter. Then I rewrote it, again and again and again. I still don't know if I hit the perfect pitch, but that just may be the devil of doubt whispering in my ear. In any event, rehashing my creative angst won't change anything, and you can judge it for yourself, because this is an amended version (I removed our contact information for the sake of privacy and a few other non-essential sentences for the sake of clarity) of the letter that I finally mailed:

Dear Mr Watterson,
    My name is Nevin Martell and I have long been an avid fan of your work. I am writing to you now, however, as not only a fan but an author as well. I am writing a book about

you and your work, and wish to secure an interview with you. I know of and respect the decisions you've made with regard to your privacy. It is with this knowledge that I lay my case before you in what I hope is the most non-invasive way possible.

I have already interviewed a number of your friends, colleagues and contemporaries so this may not be the first time you're hearing of this project. Regardless of whether or not you have heard about my efforts, I encourage you to ask the people I have interviewed about my intentions, manner and methods. I feel certain that they would all vouch for my professionalism, politeness and dedication to getting the story right. I have not pried, knowing that such actions may compromise relationships or cross boundaries that should not be crossed under any circumstances. Unlike some writers, I do not believe that the ends justify the means nor do I act in kind. I wish to preserve something of personal and social consequence and to pay tribute to its creator, not to destroy or weaken the very same in unbridled determination.

Since I first read of *Calvin and Hobbes* as a teenager, I have been curious about its genesis and the man who drew such memorable characters into being. That you have so laconically eschewed any and all offers to merchandise or exploit the strip may seem inconceivable to some, but it is the very lack of material besides the strip itself that makes its sentiments pure. Since my youth, *Calvin and Hobbes* has remained unravaged by time and unadulterated by conspicuous overexposure. It is this seeming purity that piqued my adult curiosity.

A couple of years ago I was batting around ideas for a new book project. I had written a couple of very straightforward rock 'n' roll biographies in my early twenties for Simon & Schuster's Pocket Books imprint, but they had mostly been motivated by what I thought other people wanted to learn more about. I was incredibly unhappy during the writing of my second book about a musician named Beck, and vowed to write only about what profoundly interested me. I started thinking about the things I loved that made me happy and that I didn't know much about, and that's when I realized that you and your work were largely undiscovered territory.

The book is intended to be a serious study of *Calvin and Hobbes* as I explore the strip's success as a pop culture phenomenon and its enduring influence. I promise I will forgo the kind of fanboy blathering that litters the blogosphere, though it won't be without warmth and humor.

I know you have made few forays into the public eye since the strip's retirement, and I understand that you may have some natural hesitance in talking with me. I assure you that I am an excellent interviewer who does his research and can feel out his subject's boundaries. I'd be happy to do the interview in whatever way was best for you — in person, over the phone, via email, carrier pigeon, with tin cans connected by string — and with whatever parameters you need to feel comfortable.

Come what may, it has been a rare privilege to embark on this project and I expect that I will do you and your work justice. *Calvin and Hobbes* helped shape my worldview and developed in me an appreciation for humor and wit. Reading the strips again and revisiting them with people who hold them in similar esteem has been awesome. I've found myself laughing at the antics of Calvin and Hobbes, and thinking about the larger implications of their behavior. It is a rare skill that can provoke such a reaction in many, and I appreciate the countless times you've done that for me.

Thanks so much for taking the time to read this letter and your consideration of my request for an interview. I have enclosed all of my contact information below, and I hope to talk to you further on this matter.

Even though I was happy with the letter I wrote, I was still hesitant about actually mailing it to Watterson. My reservations were born of overactive perfectionism and fear of rejection. Okay, okay, so it was mostly a fear of rejection, but I knew this book was going to consume my life and I didn't want to blow it with my star subject.

I sent the letter Priority Mail with delivery confirmation and anxiously checked and rechecked the US Postal Service website to see if it had been received like an OCD kid on crack. Three days later — after the page refreshed for what must have been the thousandth time and delivery was confirmed — I sat back and waited, though no less anxiously. I felt like Calvin after he had mailed away for the cereal premium prize, a beanie with a propeller on top, only to be told, "Please allow 4–6 weeks for your package to arrive." I mean, you might as well tell Calvin, or an adult writer named Nevin, that it'll be here in infinity times forever.

I eagerly flipped through the mail every day, hoping to see a Cleveland postmark or an envelope with Calvin and Hobbes on it, like Watterson used to use when responding to fan mail. But this virtual surveying of the horizon didn't end at the mailbox. I would scan new cars parked on my street and suspiciously check out passing pedestrians, imagining Watterson had decided to answer the letter in person. And every time the phone rang with an unfamiliar number I picked it up excitedly, imagining that Watterson had chosen to reach out to me using the phone number I had included in the letter. Weeks passed, but nothing happened. I chewed my fingers, slept poorly and developed heavy bags under my eyes that looked as if they were about to head out on a globe-circling adventure.

One day — finally — an unfamiliar Cleveland area number did come up on the phone early one morning. All of these disjointed thoughts ran riot through my head: Really? Now? I hadn't even had my second cup of coffee, I couldn't record conversations on my iPhone but I also couldn't let the call go to voicemail . . . so I got a grip and picked up.

"Hello, this is Nevin Martell," I tried to say in my coolest and most professional tone, knowing full well that I sounded neither cool nor particularly professional. "Hello, Nevin," a gravelly but warm voice replied. My head spun and in my mind's eye I saw glorious fireworks exploding all around me in celebration of my victory as the Flaming Lips song "Do You Realize??" played on a quadraphonic stereo at an ear-jarring volume.

But wait, something wasn't right. "This is Harvey Pekar," the voice continued. What? Did he just say Harvey Pekar? The fireworks stopped instantaneously and the psychedelic pop fell silent. For the smallest of seconds, my disappointment danced unchecked through my mind and on my heart. Then the rational part of my brain kicked the idiotic part, screaming, "Harvey frickin' Pekar is on the phone! That's damn cool!"

As it turned out, the *American Splendor* cartoonist had called to say that he was flattered that I had asked for his opinions on *Calvin and Hobbes* and Watterson, but didn't feel as though he could contribute. He went on to wish me good luck in my remaining interviews and writing. Now that's class. By the time I got off the phone, my excitement was once again at full throttle. Sure, it wasn't Bill Watterson, and sure Harvey Pekar didn't feel like he'd be a good interview for the book, but it was inspiring that part of the universe was acknowledging and responding to my efforts.

A similar high point was the postcard I got from England a week or two after that confidence-bolstering call. On the front was a picture of Raymond Pettibon's ink painting of a question mark and the back held this short handwritten note:

> Dear Nevin,
>
>   I'm sorry to disappoint you, but I have never in my life read a *Calvin and Hobbes* comic strip. There are people I know who love it — my brother-in-law, for instance — but I've never been a reader of the funny pages.
>   Sincerely,
>   David Sedaris

David Sedaris just sent me a postcard! I still have it on my desk, next to an old issue of a *Space Family Robinson: Lost in Space* comic book and a series of small toys I've gotten from inside Kinder Surprise chocolate eggs. Again, it didn't matter that he was saying he couldn't be of help; it was still a responsive shout from the void.

That isn't to say that I was only getting rejections, because it wasn't the case at all. During this time I interviewed everyone from

Watterson's editor Lee Salem and *Garfield* cartoonist Jim Davis to *Pearls Before Swine* creator Stephan Pastis. I also extensively interviewed an old friend of Watterson's from college, Richard West. Aside from Salem, he was one of the few people I had spoken to who still kept in touch with Watterson. Maybe I would be able to feel him out on the subject of the letter I had sent, to see if he might have any insights. I wanted to clarify a few points from our first interview, so this was a perfect excuse to get him on the phone again.

As I followed up on some questions that arose from our first interview, I managed to bite my tongue and not press West about Watterson's reaction to my letter. I assumed that West had mentioned our first conversation to Watterson, which would have alerted him to the possibility of my contacting him. However, that wasn't the case. "Your letter was news to him," West told me. "And he's not sure what the point is about talking about *Calvin and Hobbes* again," he added. I felt as if my heart were being trampled by a herd of rabid wildebeests. While I knew that Watterson hadn't given an interview in almost 20 years, and that securing an interview would be tantamount to catching the Loch Ness Monster with a 5-pound fishing line, I had still imagined — against all evidence to the contrary — that it would happen.

Unaware of the wildebeests tattooing my heart with their hooves, West kept talking, "We've had long debates — since I'm the historian and he's the artist — about the value of art history. At one point he took the position that the art is all that matters and who cares what the artist's story is. As in, you can look at a Rembrandt and appreciate a Rembrandt without knowing a single thing about Rembrandt's life. And my argument back to him is that people are drawn to genius and that they want to have a better understanding of what creates greatness. Plus, an artist's story gives a texture and meaning to the human effort. Whatever Bill decides about cooperating, it's not going to be personal."

Did he just say what I thought I heard? Be still my beating, sorely battered heart! If Watterson hadn't decided yet, it meant that he hadn't said no! Plan A — Watterson agreeing to my interview and making this whole process infinitely easier — was still a possibility.

While I clung tenuously to this possibility, I had long ago admitted to myself that it was improbable that Plan A would ever take effect because Watterson would say no to any intrusion into his self-imposed solitude. I had planned accordingly. According to Plan B — otherwise known as the Morbidly Realistic Plan — I was going to write the book as if Watterson were dead.

No matter what I discovered at the end, the search itself was going to be a globetrotting expedition of mythical proportions. I was Tintin trying to track down the yeti, Indiana Jones seeking out the Ark of the Covenant or a *National Enquirer* reporter hunting for Elvis. It was an incredibly daunting task, but I can honestly say it ended up being one of the most rewarding experiences in my life as an author. *Looking for Calvin and Hobbes* is the culmination of a year-long journey to find Bill Watterson and figure out what made him tick. I hope you enjoy retracing my steps as much as I enjoyed taking them.

CHAPTER 1

Working on a Dream

I've seen Watterson's editorial cartoons and I'm glad he went
on to do a comic strip instead.
— Pat Oliphant, Pulitzer Prize-winning editorial cartoonist

Luckily for me, the story of William Boyd Watterson II began only
a few miles away from where I sit typing this. Watterson was born
at 8:26 a.m. on 5 July 1958 at the George Washington University
Hospital in Washington, DC. His mother, Kathryn Ann Bechtel,
was 24 and his father, James Godfrey Watterson, was a 25-year-old
patent examiner for the Department of Commerce. A year and a half
later, in January 1960, his mother gave birth to a brother, Thomas.

The family of four lived just across the Potomac River in picturesque Alexandria, Virginia. Almost 200 years old and littered with
historical landmarks and placards that proclaim "Somebody famous
slept here," Alexandria has always retained an affluent small-town
vibe. Despite its proximity to the capital and a surging population
that was about 90,000 in the late 1950s, it never seemed city-like.
It was full of Mom 'n' Pop shops and people who looked as if they
had just stepped out of a Norman Rockwell painting or a Garrison
Keillor story. The town was populated by fathers who worked for

the government or for the military in some capacity, but Alexandria still had a strong backbone of blue-collar workers.

The Wattersons had an apartment in a white-painted brick house situated on one of the quiet suburban streets that gave Alexandria its quaint, colonial charm. I drove by one afternoon on the way to a friend's barbecue and snapped a few photos of it. I hoped that someone would come out and ask what I was doing so I could exchange some Watterson trivia with them. Sadly, the inhabitants were either not home, unaware or uncaring, so I had to settle with regaling my wife with some choice factoids. Since Watterson has yet to be blogged about by Perez Hilton or shown on TMZ.com, this conversational gambit was greeted with a less than enthusiastic response and I quickly changed the topic.

There is a paucity of information about this part of Watterson's life. There are scattered references to it throughout his few interviews and there are brief notes in the public records office, but nothing to give someone a sense of his day-to-day life. In a way, it's fitting that someone who turned out to be such a mystery left such an invisible trail from his birth onwards, almost as if he knew that one day he'd want to cover his tracks and melt back into obscurity.

The Watterson family lived in Alexandria until 1965 when Bill was six, at which point James and Kathryn moved their brood to Chagrin Falls, Ohio, a suburb southeast of Cleveland. Here is where Bill Watterson's story becomes easier to uncover. The family bought a small, dark cream one-story house, where Bill's parents still live today. Both parents were originally Ohioans and they were eager to be close to their families. Kathryn had been to Chagrin Falls before and the small town had always seemed to her like a good place to raise children. Though no one knew it at the time, this two-word poem on the map would become the birthplace of *Calvin and Hobbes.*

To this day, Chagrin Falls retains its classic small-town charm and Midwestern appeal. The houses and storefronts look as if they could form the backdrop of a Hollywood film set, which it actually did for 1977's made-for-TV movie *The Gathering*, a holiday redemption flick starring Ed Asner. Much of the main downtown architecture hasn't changed much in the past century and the park at the center of the town has a nineteenth-century-styled bandstand in the center of it. Though residents initially made their livings from the mills that lined the Chagrin Falls River, it had developed into a middle-class suburb by the time the Wattersons arrived.

This small burg has a proud artistic tradition, attributable in a large part to Henry Church Jr, a painter and stone carver from the 1800s. His most famous work is a 30-foot high rock sculpture next to the Chagrin River, which is publicly referred to as "Squaw Rock," though the artist's formal name for the piece was "The Rape of the Indian Tribes by the White Man." (Mini-replicas of this piece are available as favors for children's birthday parties!) Ohio as a whole has an incredibly rich artistic legacy, especially when it comes to cartooning. There are over a hundred cartoonists who grew up in the state or called it their home at one point or another, including Milton Caniff (*Terry and the Pirates, Steve Canyon*), Cathy Guisewite (*Cathy*) and Winsor McCay (*Little Nemo in Slumberland*). Though the Wattersons didn't move there because of this artistic legacy, it would prove to be fertile ground for their young son.

According to his parents, Bill was not a rambunctious kid. "He was a conservative child," his father James Watterson told the *Cleveland Plain Dealer.* "Not that he was unimaginative, because of course he was. But not in a fantasy way." Bill and Tom would make time-lapse movies—"But he was nothing like Calvin," James Watterson asserted in the same article. "He didn't have an imaginary friend like Hobbes and he wasn't a Dennis the Menace." His mother confirmed this in a separate interview: "Calvin was a pretty raucous kid and Bill was a pretty quiet kid." One thing Bill and Calvin did have in common was a love of sledding. There is a big hill in the Watterson's backyard, which Bill and his brother would go zipping down during Ohio's long winter months. Clearly, it was an activity that made a deep impression on him, because it would become one of Watterson's most beloved go-to storytelling devices in *Calvin and Hobbes*.

Through a contact at the Chagrin Falls Alumni Association, I was introduced to a former classmate and longtime friend of Watterson's, David Bowe. Now a doctor, but still living in the town where he grew up, Bowe moved to Chagrin Falls in 1968 when he was in fourth grade. Watterson made a strong first impression on him. "Nobody knew who I was, I was the new kid," Bowe told me. "He was really popular, because he could draw and nobody else could do that." Bowe still owns a colored pencil drawing Watterson gave him of a scene from Disney's *The Jungle Book* from that time. He knew then that they would be friends for a very long time.

It was at this juncture that Watterson first started reading cartoons. His father owned some Schulz collections, which became some of the first books he ever read. "One book was called *Snoopy*, and it had a blank title page," Watterson later told an audience at the Festival of Cartoon Art. "The next page had a picture of Snoopy. I apparently figured the publisher had supplied the blank title page as a courtesy so the reader could use it to trace the drawing of Snoopy underneath. I added my own frontispiece to my dad's book. And afterward my dad must not have wanted the book back because I still have it." From then on, the young comic-strip fan bought the annual *Peanuts* collections and used them as a home-school course in cartooning, "with the idea of someday becoming the next Charles Schulz," he later told the *Wall Street Journal*.

"At that time, most of [*Peanuts*] went over my head," he admitted to an interviewer in 1987. "I certainly had no understanding of how revolutionary *Peanuts* was or how it was changing the comics." What he did know was that he worshipped the strip and its creator. When he was in fourth grade, Watterson wrote a letter to Schulz. To his surprise, the cartoonist wrote back. ". . . I still have that letter," he told the *Cleveland Plain Dealer* in 1986. "It made a big impression on me at the time." Encouraged by his hero's correspondence, Watterson wrote Schulz another fan letter — and received the same form letter as he had the first time. It must have been a sobering moment to get a glimpse of how the world really works, but it didn't prevent the young Watterson from forever loving *Peanuts*.

Watterson made another influential cartooning discovery a couple of years later when he picked up a used copy of Walt Kelly's *The Pogo Papers* at a library book sale for a quarter. He bought it with the intention of giving it to his father as a gift, but as soon as he started reading it, his father lost a gift and the young Watterson gained a new love. "The humor and the artwork were what first attracted me," he admitted to an audience at the Ohio State University in 1988. "But those things are the colorful sugar coating on the medicine," he continued. "The medicine is that *Pogo* is about something . . . *Pogo* talked about the quiet dignity and common sense of average man . . . the shortcomings of human nature . . . suspicion and prejudice, pollution and the bomb. It also celebrated silliness, nonsense and the simple pleasure of a big picnic. It talked about friendship and love, our strange political system, baseball, and hundreds of other things great and small." He was hooked on the art of cartooning.

Watterson started to devote a lot of his spare time to learning how to draw. "My little comics were a natural way to depict the things I thought about at that time, such as *Batman* and how annoying my brother was," Watterson later wrote. His family was very encouraging of his artistic streak; his parents bought him a drawing table, while his mother constantly volunteered to be his test audience of one. By seventh grade, Watterson knew that this was what he wanted to do professionally. "I wanted to be either a cartoonist or an astronaut," he joked years later, in the introduction to *The Complete Calvin and Hobbes*. "The latter was never much of a possibility, as I don't even like riding in elevators."

Cartooning was a full-time passion for Watterson, who took every chance he had to draw. Watterson collaborated on a number of cartoons for German class with Bowe, who remembers one strip in particular. The two friends were superheroes; Watterson was Waterman and Bowe was Brownie Man. "Because I was the good student, I had a brown outfit," Bowe good-naturedly recounted. "His character had a blue-green, cool-looking water-themed outfit with spandex." Though the storylines were made up of high-school twists on classic comic-book conventions — battling legions of evil teachers and changing into their costumes in the men's bathroom — the strip was markedly different from your usual *Marvel* fare. "Instead of "pow" it was "pau," because we had to do the sound effects in German," Bowe remembered with a chuckle. "I always thought it was funnier because you had to work hard to get the jokes, too."

Watterson also conceived a strip called *Raumfahrer Rolf* (Spaceman Rolf), which followed an embryonic Spaceman Spiff character on an adventure that ends poorly when he is consumed by a monster. Though this was a very early, primitive version of the alter ego he would go on to create for Calvin, it's nonetheless the beginning of something far greater than Watterson realized at the time.

This wasn't the only chance he had to show off his drawing skills. In high school he wrote a paper entitled "Drawings of Chagrin: Buildings in the downtown area — late 1800s and present," which the Chagrin Falls Historical Society now has on deposit. Watterson wrote a short essay and accompanied it with a series of sketches that compared a handful of structures' façades in downtown Chagrin Falls — the bank, the pharmacy, the town hall and others — in their incarnations in two time periods. The precise line drawings were rendered with an architectural fastidiousness that earned the young artist an "AAA Excellent."

The people that I spoke with who knew Watterson during this time characterize him as outgoing with his friends, but otherwise reserved. "He has charisma, but you have to get to know him to see it," Bowe told me. "I wouldn't say he's awkward, but he's a little averse to attention. He can handle himself; he just doesn't like it." I tracked down a few of Watterson's teachers, including Bill Foley, the high-school band director, who confirmed Bowe's characterization. "He was quiet," Foley said to me in a phone interview. "A real pleasant kid, but not at all boisterous. I'd say he was on the shy side."

Despite this shyness, Watterson had a close group of friends who called themselves the Moosers. The group included Bowe, as well as some other friends from Watterson's neighborhood, John Baker and brothers Brad and Jeffrey Toole. They formed a make-believe volleyball team, and though they never competed, they did make up T-shirts. Years later, Watterson dedicated *The Authoritative Calvin and Hobbes* to these friends, bringing his cartoon childish wonder back full circle to the friends he experienced it with when he was a kid.

Academically, Watterson did well. He was a good student, earning a membership in the National Honor Society and getting nominated his junior year for a writing award. In an article in the school paper, the *Valley Lantern*, Watterson quipped, "Pshaw! It wasn't anything any other red-blooded, all-American boy couldn't have done." Watterson actually contributed to the *Valley Lantern* as a cartoonist his junior and senior years. The first of these cartoons I uncovered was from the 20 February 1975 issue and shows an inmate caught in a spotlight as he tries escaping over a barbed-wire-topped wall. Watterson drew at least eight pieces of cartoon art for the *Lantern*, mostly small vignettes lampooning stereotypical high-school characters. None of these figures look anything like his *Calvin and Hobbes* characters, but his sketch of the school mascot was a surprising discovery. That's because the Chagrin Falls team is — would you believe it — the Tigers. Watterson drew the mascot on at least one occasion for the *Lantern*, though his renderings of the giant feline never approached the grace and artistry of Hobbes.

His senior year, Watterson uncharacteristically auditioned for a role in the drama club's production of *Stage Door*, the play by Edna Ferber and George S. Kaufman. To everyone's surprise, not only did he get a part — he got the lead. He had done some skit comedy at the school talent show, the *Orange and Black Review*, but this starring role was an unexpected coup. I uncovered a few black-and-white pictures of the production in the yearbook, the

Zenith, including one of Watterson on stage looking far more confident than his acquaintances' characterizations made him out to be. Though he may have been shy, he was certainly involved. He worked on the yearbook his senior year by contributing the cover art and a slew of cartoons for the interior. Like his work for the *Lantern*, these cartoons mostly sought to capture the people he saw walking around the halls every day. Considering there are at least 20 of Watterson's works scattered throughout the yearbook, it feels almost like his portfolio.

Watterson's senior year picture in the *Zenith* shows a smiling young man with '70s-style curled brown hair that stretches towards his shoulders, but doesn't quite make it. Dressed in a suit and tie and wearing a pair of big, square glasses, he looks very much the part of the earnest young man. He lists his nicknames as Wassersohn and, simply, Bill. The rest of his inscription is made up of short inside jokes — "Pshaw! . . . Mooser . . . Deutsch IV . . . Aarrroooo" — but ends with one prescient word: "cartoons."

Things were already looking up for him in that department. His final year at Chagrin Falls High, he submitted an editorial cartoon to the local *Sun Herald* newspaper, which, much to his astonishment and delight, they published. Not only that, but the editors liked the work so much that they encouraged Watterson to continue submitting cartoons, an unprecedented accomplishment for a high-school student.

In that spring of 1976, Watterson drew a lighthearted cartoon for his fellow seniors to immortalize their upcoming graduation. A mop-topped guy with his eyes obscured by hair muses, "Gee, in ten years, I'll probably have a job, my own car, maybe a house, a wife . . . who knows, maybe I'll even have kids!" He gives himself his own punch line, "Nahhh, not me! I'll never be twenty-eight!"

Watterson was voted the "Most Artistic" by his classmates in the superlatives issue of the school paper the spring he graduated. The accompanying picture shows the spectacled artist pretending to be caught in the act of spray-painting his name on a brick wall. I wonder how often those superlatives turn out to be true. Like, what happened to Sandra Wiper, the girl standing next to Watterson, who was also voted the "Most Artistic"? Probably having drinks with the "Most Likely To Succeed" and "The Biggest Flirt" while listening to "Glory Days."

By the time he graduated, Watterson was involved with a local girl, Melissa Richmond, the daughter of the assistant principal of the high school. Known as "Missy" to her friends, band director Bill Foley remembers her as a quiet girl. "She was just very focused and bright," Foley told me. "She did what she needed to do and was very responsible, but definitely on the quiet side."

Though he had made up his mind that cartooning was the course he wanted to follow, Watterson had decided to attend Kenyon College. This was due in part to their strong poli-sci reputation, a major he felt might be a good stepping stone for him to try out editorial cartooning. But this move downstate was not going to be the end of his fledgling relationship with Melissa, who would be attending Kent State University. In fact, the groundwork he laid in high school would be the beginning of many things that wouldn't come to fruition for another decade.

A small liberal arts college, Kenyon has a gorgeous 1,000-acre setting on a hilltop in Gambier, Ohio, about an hour's drive northeast of Columbus. Known as much for its beautiful campus as for its academics, Kenyon boasts that it is the only college to include a former prime minister and former president in their alumni ranks — Olof Palme, prime minister of Sweden from 1982–6, graduated in 1948, while Rutherford B. Hayes graduated back in 1842. Though pop junkies fixate on alums like Paul Newman and *The West Wing*'s Allison Janney, Kenyon may be best known for its literary-minded grads, including celebrated novelists E. L. Doctorow and William Gass, and Pulitzer Prize-winning poets Robert Lowell and James Wright.

The first week of his freshman year, Watterson fortuitously met Rich West, then a senior, and managing editor of the school paper, the *Kenyon Collegian*. West has gone on to become a comic historian of no small distinction and owns a rare magazine shop in Easthampton, Massachusetts, called Periodyssey, where I tracked him down in the summer of 2008. My subsequent telephone conversations and email discussions with West, perhaps the most vocal and knowledgeable of Watterson's confidants, helped reveal an intriguing picture of the young cartoonist.

West remembers meeting Watterson at a fair that was designed to introduce incoming freshmen to campus organizations. "He was a tentative, modest guy," West told me. Watterson had gravitated towards the *Collegian*'s table, where West was working. The freshman had discovered that Jim Borgman, who had graduated that spring, was already working for the *Cincinnati Enquirer* as a political cartoonist. Borgman had worked at the *Collegian* and "Watterson found this to be an exciting development," West recounts. "Number one: that anyone could make money drawing cartoons. And number two: that he was close to ground zero of someone who had actually done it."

Borgman went on to work for the *Enquirer* full-time for over 30 years and created the comic strip *Zits* with Jerry Scott, which follows the misadventures of 15-year-old wannabe rock star Jeremy Duncan and his adolescent travails. I tracked Borgman down through the paper and he was kind enough to agree to fit in an email interview between his impressive comic workload. He remembers being more shocked than anyone that editorial cartooning might be a career path. "My dad was a sign painter and all the dads in my neighborhood fixed cars, drove trucks or installed siding for a living," Borgman wrote in an email. "I didn't know there were jobs where you didn't get dirty and sweaty." Watterson was so encouraged by the notion that cartooning was a viable way of making a living that he immediately signed on to be the political cartoonist for the *Collegian*. Since Borgman had graduated, no one else had expressed an interest in the position, so Watterson was drawing cartoons for the paper within his first month.

"Political cartooning seemed like a profitable outlet for my cartooning," Watterson later admitted to the *Collegian*. "[F]reshman year I had no real understanding of the political world." For Watterson, this was a means to an end. "He hadn't actually aspired to political cartooning," West concurred. "His interest had always been comic strips."

Since Watterson was relatively inexperienced, he and West worked together on his initial contributions. Every week they would meet to discuss the issues that might form the basis for a cartoon and how they might translate on the page. "I guess you could say it was a tutorial in political cartooning," West quipped to me. It was not a match made in heaven, though. "Our collaborations were terrible," he admitted with a chuckle. "I'm not an artist, so I couldn't necessarily translate my ideas into effective drawings, and because Bill didn't originate the idea he simply tried to create something that wasn't his. It didn't really work."

After a while, the duo gave up this approach and Watterson took sole ownership of his work. West still offered occasional advice by mail after he graduated at the end of Watterson's freshman year, as did Jim Borgman. "This flattered me into pursuing a career for which I had neither the brains nor the talent," Watterson later joked in the foreword to Borgman's *Disturbing the Peace* collection. "That ruined several years of my life, and I still hold Jim responsible for it."

Watterson also found the time to ink a comic strip entitled *Mewkis and Fester* for the paper. "It was just this side of objectionable," West laughingly recounts. The strip revolves around a pair of roommates: Mewkis, a chunkier kid with thin hair; and Fester, a slim poli-sci major with messy, short hair and a stubbly hint of a moustache. Comparing Fester to pictures of Watterson from that period reveals that the comic college kid is at least partially a lampoon of the artist himself.

Mewkis and Fester are a far cry visually from Calvin and Hobbes, but the duos actually have a lot in common. Both sets of friends love to avoid schoolwork, get into trouble constantly and have an innate distaste for authority. Three *Mewkis and Fester* strips I was able to dig up in the Kenyon library are particularly evocative of the spirit of *Calvin and Hobbes*, including the strip from the 25 January 1979 issue, in which Mewkis spills a beer, kick-starting a food fight that's reminiscent of the strips in which Calvin literally fights with his food. In another "*Calvin* moment," Fester is daydreaming in poli-sci class, before creating a ruckus by coughing out a commentary, "AH … AH … AHH … AHHORSHT! AHBULSHT!" In the final panel,

Fester is at the chalkboard in a very Bart Simpson-esque manner, writing over and over again, "I will not create a disturbance in class." It reminds me of the moments when Calvin is sent to the corner or the principal's office and he comes out of his reveries only to find himself about to be disciplined.

A final moment of particular *Calvin*-ism is from the 1 November 1979 issue, when the twosome are racing to finish kegs, before Mewkis reminds Fester he has an econ paper due the next morning. Fester manages to churn out a 15-page research paper in just four and a half hours with the help of a massive caffeine overload. The strip ends with his handing in a paper written in gibberish, as he gleefully and ignorantly skips away yelling, "This calls for celebration!" Calvin often took great delight in sub-par work he thought was excellent, though it's hard to imagine him doing a keg stand to celebrate turning that work in.

Despite these specific examples, the most obvious parallel is that both sets of characters have to interact with the academic world, often with disastrous results. Calvin is routinely disciplined, fails to grasp even simple arithmetic and is frequently bullied, while Mewkis and Fester can hardly get out of bed, party whenever possible and have a singular lack of dedication to their schoolwork. In a sense, all of these characters yearn for an eternal summer where there are no deadlines, bedtimes or rules. I couldn't agree with them more. After all, why should we survive on just two weeks of vacation a year when life can be an extraordinary vacation?

Two of Watterson's closest friends at Kenyon were Tom Tenney and Tom Chesnutt. Chesnutt would go on to be the only friend of Bill's to get his name in *Calvin and Hobbes*. In the lone strip, Calvin's mother asks him whether he's going to bring Hobbes to school and whether the kids make fun of him for it. "Tommy Chesnutt did once, and now nobody does," Calvin retorts. "Why, what happened to Tommy Chesnutt?" his mother queries. "Hobbes ate him!" Calvin replies, as Hobbes makes a disgusted face and quips, "Ugh! He needed a bath, too . . ."

Watterson and his two friends anonymously collaborated on a column for the *Collegian* under the pseudonym Pee Wee Fernbuster. The topics ranged from the ridiculous to the utterly ridiculous, including one column about how to do multiple term papers in one short weekend. It's an issue close to my heart even now (this sentence was written under deadline) and Fernbuster doles out some good advice, including "You can always make a quote relevant to your theme if you try," "[B]e sure to choose a topic that is flexible enough to be used for all your classes," and "If you suspect your professor just reads the first and last pages of your papers, sheets of copper can be stolen from the art department and pasted between two pages for that "weighty feeling.""

Not all of the Pee Wee Fernbuster columns were as funny as the term paper advice column. There is a series from the spring semester of Watterson's junior year that takes potshots at the short-lived editor-in-chief, Cynthia Savage. Written in all caps, the column devolves from an attack on Savage to a condemnation of all women on campus. Kenyon, like my alma mater, Vassar, went co-ed in '69 and it's clear that Pee Wee still hadn't adjusted to the idea. "BY DEMANDING THE SAME ACADEMIC STANDARDS FOR THE ACCEPTANCE OF WOMEN AS FOR MEN, KENYON ATTRACTS MORE THAN ITS SHARE OF UGLY GIRLS," Pee Wee blusters. "IT'S SELF EVIDENT THAT THE ONLY GIRLS WHO COULD HAVE PUT IN THE EXTRA STUDY TIME NECESSARY TO EQUAL THE

MEN'S PERFORMANCE, AND THUS BE ADMITTED, WERE THE GIRLS WHO WERE TOO UGLY TO GET DATES IN HIGH SCHOOL."

Later in the same essay, Pee Wee proclaims, "I KNOW A *LOT* ABOUT WOMEN, I READ *HUSTLER*," before concluding, "WOMEN HAVE TWO APPROPRIATE PLACES IN TODAY'S SOCIETY. ONE IS IN THE KITCHEN." Frankly, if anyone had ever published that at Vassar they would have been hung, drawn, quartered, set on fire, thrown in acid, shot and then lynched in front of the president's house. Actually, it never would have made it into the paper, but one can imagine. It's impossible to tell which of the three friends wrote this particular column, so there's no assigning responsibility for it. Thankfully, *Calvin and Hobbes* never included anything blatantly sexist, though *Rhymes With Orange* cartoonist Hilary Price later pointed out to me that Susie Derkins is hardly a post-modern feminist, with her stereotypical love of stuffed bunny rabbits, tea parties and playing house. She does compensate for this classic girlishness by occasionally nailing Calvin with a snowball, which elevates her far above a mere cutout of a character and gives her some real heft.

Though Watterson was a poli-sci major, he did take a number of art classes. One of his drawing teachers, Martin Garhart, remembers him as a smart, but stubborn, student. "He wanted to do cartoons for practically every assignment," Garhart revealed to me when I caught up with him in his studio in Wyoming. "But when he broke away from that he was an excellent classical drawer, too." Garhart is now retired from teaching at Kenyon, but he kept up with Watterson for years after his student graduated. Now Garhart paints full-time and his works have hung all over the world, including in the Library of Congress and the British Museum. After we talked, he referred me to another professor of Watterson's, Joseph Slate, who taught Watterson for both Intermediate and Advanced Drawing.

After teaching at Kenyon for years, Slate went on to become an acclaimed children's author, penning the much-adored *Miss Bindergarten* series. He just so happens to live a few miles away with me in Silver Spring, Maryland, and was easy to track down. (If only Watterson were so easy!) He had recently published a new book, *I Want to be Free*, but generously made time in his schedule to share his few memories of Watterson. "The talent was there, but he had not yet let Calvin out, or maybe was not sure Calvin was even in him," Slate told me. "Isn't that always the problem with anyone in the creative arts? You keep searching for the idea that liberates your talent." Though he and Watterson have never spoken since college, Slate received an autographed copy of *The Essential Calvin and Hobbes* out of the blue almost a decade later.

When he wasn't drawing cartoons in class or for the paper, Watterson continued to draw editorial cartoons and spot art for the *Sun Herald* chain, which earned him an honorable mention in a National Newspaper Association contest in 1977. Sometimes these cartoons tackled serious political issues like school levies and the under-equipping of the local fire department, but he more often dealt with lighter fare; one strip was a miniature board game and another a Calvin-esque poem dedicated to the joys of spring, while two others borrowed poems from fellow Ohioan Marie Daerr Boehringer to celebrate Thanksgiving and New Year's Eve.

The *Sun Herald* also published the first ever interview with the burgeoning cartoonist on 12 January 1978. Entitled "*Herald* cartoonist says it ain't easy," Watterson contributed a portrait of himself at his drawing table, hands stained with ink and a pile of crumpled-up ideas behind him. On the wall behind him hangs a calendar with Snoopy as the Red Baron on top of his doghouse.

"Getting the ideas is the painful part," Watterson confessed. "The drawing is the fun part." According to the artist, it took him three to six hours to do the drawing and just as long to come up with the idea for it. "I spend hours in my room just leafing through magazines and newspapers looking for a good analogy," he revealed. "Then [I] begin to play round with it. Sometimes it is very difficult. Other times, it comes quickly." No matter what subject he's tackling, Watterson wanted to make sure that he always had an opinion. "I don't want to do greeting cards," he declared. "I don't want to just illustrate a situation. Anyone can do that. I want to make a definite statement in a fair and humorous way. I think that in my best cartoons, I have achieved that." Even early on, Watterson wanted his cartoons to make an impact and cause people to think.

Bowe remembers the letters he got from Watterson during this time. "He would normally draw on the envelope," Bowe told me. "There would be a hilarious, ridiculous-looking, very elaborate picture on most of it. His letters talked about what classes he was taking and what he was doing, but he always had the funniest way of putting it. Those letters were like gold."

Despite a full academic and extracurricular slate, Watterson still found time to goof off. In his sophomore year he painted Michelangelo's "Creation of Adam" from the Sistine Chapel on the ceiling of his dorm room. Some friends helped rig scaffolding for him by stacking two chairs on top of his bed and laying a table across them, which brought him within 2 feet of his canvas. He drew a grid on the ceiling and used his art history book as a guide.

"I wasn't much of a painter then," Watterson admitted later. "But what the work lacked in color sense and technical flourish, it gained in the incongruity of having a High Renaissance masterpiece in a college dorm that had the unmistakable odor of old beer cans and older laundry. The painting lent an air of cosmic grandeur to my room, and it seemed to put life into a larger perspective. Those boring, flowery English poets didn't seem quite so important, when right above my head God was transmitting the spark of life to man."

Perhaps the funniest part of this odd little tale is that Watterson had failed to ask for permission before painting this mural, and then decided to apply retroactively. "[Y]ou don't get to be a sophomore at Kenyon without learning how to fabricate ideas you never had," Watterson quipped. Though the housing director realized what had happened, Watterson was allowed to paint the picture — or, rather, keep what had already been painted — as long as he painted over it at the end of the year. So, a few weeks later he found himself covering up the project that had consumed the previous two semesters.

By the time Watterson was a senior, his life was a whirlwind of cartooning. In addition to his multiple obligations at the *Collegian* and his *Sun Herald* freelance gig, Watterson took time to ink the cover of *The Best Political Cartoons of 1978*, which was edited by his old friend Rich West. Watterson's piece showed a hand inking the title of the book onto a blank page. He also contributed a number of his *Collegian* editorial cartoons to the yearbook, the *Reveille*. Unfortunately, several of them are presented with their colors in reverse, so they look like negatives of his original strips. According to people I talked with, Watterson was livid over this mistake, though you wouldn't be able to tell that from his grinning senior picture.

He's got John Lennon's glasses, Scott Baio in *Joanie Loves Chachi*'s haircut, and Tom Selleck's moustache from *Magnum, P. I.*, while he holds what looks like a Siamese cat. His exuberant picture shares the page with those of his Pee Wee Fernbuster co-conspirators, Tom Tenney and Tommy Chesnutt. (I tried contacting both of Watterson's old college friends, but neither returned my requests for an interview.)

By the time the *Reveille* was published in the spring of 1980, Watterson had accumulated an impressive portfolio. A retrospective of the work, "The Worst of Watterson," was displayed in the last days of April his senior year. Most of the pieces in the exhibit were culled from his last two years. "I think I only had one cartoon from freshman year in the show," Watterson told the *Collegian*. "I did a lot of really terrible ones that year — real junk. I can hardly stand to look at anything I did before my junior year." The article was accompanied by a self-portrait: Watterson sitting at his desk in a room full of empty bottles and a poster of the Ayatollah Khomeini. The lanky artist is wearing a wife-beater and shorts decorated with the Playboy logo, while a thought bubble floats above him, filled with nothing but an asterisk.

Though he had to put in long hours to fulfill his many comic strip obligations, his cartooning work had gotten him noticed off campus. John Smale, chairman of the Kenyon Board of Trustees, was a fan — and a friend of the editor of the *Cincinnati Post*. He brought the editor some of Watterson's cartoons, which impressed the editor enough to offer Watterson a six-month trial contract. "I hope the editor and I will get along," Watterson told the *Collegian*. "He said he expects me to argue for my ideas with him." He had no idea what he was getting himself into.

With four years of political cartooning under his belt at the *Collegian* and the *Sun Herald*, Watterson thought that being a political cartoonist was his dream job, but it came with a head-spinning twist. Watterson's good friend and idol, Jim Borgman, was making great strides at the *Post*'s rival, the *Cincinnati Enquirer*. "Neither of us dreamed I'd end up in the same town on the opposite paper," Watterson later told *Honk!* magazine. It was, as Watterson's friend West said, as if "lightning [had] struck twice. It was a very exciting and amazing development." But it also meant Watterson was competing against his hero.

According to Borgman, his first years with the *Enquirer* were a formative experience. "Savvy readers probably could have told you whose work I'd studied the previous night by the style they found in my cartoon the next morning," he admits now. "It's essentially the same process every good cartoonist I know has gone through, but I was doing it in public." As Borgman blossomed as an editorial cartoonist, he also became distressed. "At Kenyon, my cartoons were greeted with warm support and backslapping," he remembers. "But when I got to the *Cincinnati Enquirer* a week after graduating, I was suddenly met with angry phone callers and sharp-tongued letters to the editor. I had to grow tough skin fast and it was pretty traumatizing. I was in so far over my head I can't tell you."

Watterson later wrote an affectionate review of a collection of Borgman's work from this period for Rich West's *Target* magazine. "A casual flip through [*The Great Communicator*] shows a boggling display of approaches to each issue," Watterson opined. "Few artists are as versatile with all the tools at the cartoonist's disposal. Borgman wields the sledgehammer as confidently as the feather, and no one is more adept at the visual curve ball . . . Borgman can really draw. As he pushes his line quality in a more personal direction, there will be no stopping him."

Borgman had drawn fewer than two dozen cartoons for publication before he debuted on the daily editorial page. "It was harrowing," Borgman admits now. "But I was devoted and I had a patient editor and publisher." Unfortunately for Watterson, his parallel life was like a nightmare version of Borgman's. "My Cincinnati days were pretty Kafkaesque," Watterson told *Honk!* years later. Though he had only just moved to Cincinnati, the editor insisted that most of his work be about local, as opposed to national, issues. Since Watterson had no grasp of the local political landscape, this proved to be an ill-starred expectation. "The job was a disaster," Watterson later wrote in the introduction to *The Complete Calvin and Hobbes*. The first day would be symptomatic of this full-scale horror show. "[A]fter several rough ideas were rejected, I submitted increasingly bizarre sketches in the frantic hope of making the deadline," Watterson continued, "until the editor finally came out of his office, walked over to my desk, and told me to call it a day. It went downhill from there."

Looking back at Watterson's work from this period, you can see that it was a formative time for him. The stereotypical collegiate characters that littered his Kenyon 'toons evolved into their adult counterparts. Although they had a unifying style, it was not a singular style. However, you are able to see the genesis of *Calvin and Hobbes* in some of the disgruntled businessmen and politicians that populate the early strips; many of them look like precursors to Principal Spittle. More importantly, there's the first appearance of Calvin that I was able to find. This is not Calvin as in the character Calvin, but Calvin in his visual form. The cartoon from 17 July

1980, about a heatwave that sent Cincinnati residents into a famous local fountain for relief, has a small figure in the corner of the panel. It's a young boy with spiky blonde hair and a horizontally striped shirt. He's wearing a snorkel and mask, but his similarity to Calvin is undeniable.

Over the course of his six-month contract, Watterson had a number of cartoons published. Many of these works are still buried in Cincinnati area libraries, but I was able to track down a number of them, certainly enough to give a good representation of Watterson's output at this time. He commented on a variety of local topics — including Cincinnati public schools' decision to allow locker searches and Ohio governor Jim Rhodes's stance on the energy crisis — as well as the occasional national issue, such as Carter and Kennedy's battle for the Democratic nomination. Unfortunately, Watterson never really had a chance. "Cincinnati at that time was also beginning to realize it had major cartooning talent in Jim Borgman . . . and I didn't benefit from the comparison," Watterson told *Honk!*. "I don't know to what extent the comparison played a role in my editor's not liking my work," Watterson pondered in the same interview. "But I was very intimidated by working on a major city paper and I didn't feel free to experiment, really, or to travel down my own path."

Unfortunately, he spent most of his time trying to please his editor, not himself. "I very early caught on that the editor had something specific in mind that he was looking for, and I tried to accommodate him in order to get published," Watterson admitted in the *Honk!* interview. "His idea was that he was going to publish only my very best work so that I wouldn't embarrass the newspaper while I learned the ropes. As sound as that idea may be from the management standpoint, it was disastrous for me because I was only getting a couple cartoons a week printed. I would turn out rough idea after rough idea, and he would veto eighty percent of them. As a result, I lost all my self-confidence, and his intervention was really unhealthy, I think, as far as letting me experiment and make mistakes and become a stronger cartoonist for it."

"In a different situation, in a different town with a different editor, he could have shone as a political cartoonist," West theorizes now. "But he didn't have any breathing room in Cincinnati. Borgman sucked up a lot of the oxygen. He was the dominant cartoonist in town and Bill's editor was impatient and expected him to be Borgman. He wasn't interested in Bill developing his own voice, he wanted a Borgman Jr. That's bad to ask of any cartoonist, but it was particularly stultifying in Bill's case, because he wasn't cocky and he wasn't confident of his skills. He was as amazed as anyone when he got that job and worked very hard to try to make it happen. But when you're in a situation when you get the feeling that the people you work for have no confidence in you, it can be very demoralizing."

As the weeks ticked by, the job began to look less than a coup and more like a Pyrrhic victory for Watterson. He was becoming demoralized by the small, chronic failures that led inexorably to his unemployment. "The agreement was that they could fire me or I could quit with no questions asked if things didn't work out," Watterson told *Honk!*. "Sure enough, things didn't work out, and they fired me, no questions asked." By the end of his short tenure, Watterson wasn't even sure why they had hired him in the first place. "Obviously, if [my editor] wanted a more experienced cartoonist, he shouldn't have hired a kid just out of college," he griped in the

Honk! interview. "I pretty much prostituted myself for six months but I couldn't please [my editor], so he sent me packing."

When Watterson was let go, depression mingled with catharsis. In a way, his editor had freed him from the prison of his nascent, and ultimately crippling, expectations. On the other hand, he was out of a job and his career in political cartooning was DOA. Thus began a period of deep introspection and revelation. In describing the period following this, his first great failure, Watterson later told West during an interview for *The Comics Journal* that the "experience itself was horrible, but getting fired forced me to re-examine how committed I was to political cartooning, and I finally admitted to myself that it had always been very difficult for me. I was never really very good at it."

Watterson continued in this vein of postmortem analysis in his interview with *Honk!*: "I was never one of those people who reads the headlines and foams at the mouth with rabid opinion that I've just got to get down on paper," Watterson admitted. "I guess I just don't have the killer instinct that I think makes a great political cartoonist." There must be great truth in these conclusions because Rich West all but concurred, saying, "It's almost impossible to imagine that he could have created anything nearly as significant as a political cartoonist than he did with *Calvin and Hobbes.*"

Martin Garhart remembers Watterson coming back to Kenyon to see an exhibit Jim Borgman had around this time. Watterson was understandably depressed, but Garhart encouraged him to continue cartooning. Unfortunately for Watterson, he had not yet conceived *Calvin and Hobbes* at the time of his firing, and to pay the bills, he took a job doing layout work for a weekly publication much like the *Pennysaver*.

Time could not dull the knife of remembrance when it came to this particular job, and in a speech at Kenyon many years later Watterson still talked about it with loathing: "A real job is a job you hate," he declared. "I designed car ads and grocery ads in the windowless basement of a convenience store, and I hated every single minute of the four and a half million minutes I worked there. My fellow prisoners at work were basically concerned about how to punch the time clock at the perfect second where they would earn another twenty cents without doing any work for it. It was incredible: after every break, the entire staff would stand around in the garage where the time clock was, and wait for that last click. And after my used car needed the head gasket replaced twice, I waited in the garage, too."

Perhaps feeling that this declaration failed to say it all, Watterson went into further detail in the introduction to *The Complete Calvin and Hobbes*: "[O]ne might charitably say the boss had rage issues, so the office environment was dreary and oppressive, except when enlivened with episodes of fire-breathing insanity." To relieve the tedium of the job and perhaps to seek solace in the inanimate, Watterson would walk to a nearby cemetery and read. "It wasn't a job that Bill showed off," West says. "It was just a functional job. After the *Cincinnati Post*, where he had taken something of a beating psychologically, it was okay to just have this fairly mindless job that paid the bills, so that he had energy left over to concentrate on doing what he really wanted to do."

The fact was, he still wanted to cartoon. Luckily, he still had his hand in the game. In need of a supplemental paycheck, Watterson continued working for the *Sun* newspaper chain. He was paid $25 per cartoon, hardly a subsistence wage, but it helped him make ends meet. More importantly, though, it meant that he continued to publish cartoons. Given his somewhat ignominious ouster from the *Post* this was an ego boost he needed, albeit a humble one. As West says, "It was just to keep his hand in cartooning."

Jeff Darcy — then a colleague of Watterson's at the *Sun* and now the editorial cartoonist for the *Cleveland Plain Dealer* — remembers first seeing Watterson's work. "It seems crazy and insane to say now, but I wasn't overly impressed with them," he admits. "I'm sure people who hear that would say, "*What!??!* He's a legendary cartoonist; that's idiotic." But editorial cartoons aren't just about the art — it's about the idea. It wasn't that I didn't think his artwork was all that hot; it was the ideas it represented and the content."

Darcy was an aspiring cartoonist himself, just out of college and eager to get his career off the ground. Though Watterson's work was well liked at the *Sun*, one editor decided to take a chance on Darcy while keeping Watterson on staff. "I don't know if it was because he wasn't too crazy about Watterson's editorial cartoons or that he just saw something in my cartoons that he liked," Darcy confided. "I had done a few spec cartoons on Cleveland public schools — which is a long-standing issue in Cleveland — and he liked them. My artwork was nowhere near the level of Watterson's — it might not be at that level now," he added with a gracious laugh. Once on board, Darcy's work began running in some of the *Sun*'s papers, but it was Watterson's work that achieved the wider publication.

While Watterson was finding his professional footing, his personal life was flourishing. After courting his high-school sweetheart, Melissa Richmond, he proposed and they married on 8 October 1983; they were both 25. On their marriage license application he listed his occupation as "Layout Artist." This bureaucratic compromise must have irked the aspiring cartoonist, but the state wanted a concrete and easily ascertainable answer, not a desired occupational description.

Despite being a newlywed man with a full-time and a part-time job, Watterson was quite prolific during this period. Though West couldn't remember all of the many side projects Watterson undertook, he implied that Watterson generated a fair amount of miscellany during that time. The diverse nature of the projects Watterson participated in allowed him to flex his creative muscles and hone his cartooning skills. Two projects West does recall are a T-shirt Watterson designed for an environmental event in suburban Cleveland and a 1982 calendar, *Judy Ernest's Single-handed Survival Calendar*.

Another particularly notable side project from this era is a series of sketches Watterson drew for his college friend's father, Tom Tenney, from 1982 to 1986, when the elder Tenney was the editor of the *Mark Twain Journal*. It turns out he's still the editor, so I was able to find him through the magazine. After some back and forth, we finally talked in early August 2008. Tenney felt as if he didn't have much to tell me, though he did offer up that Watterson was a nice guy with a good sense of humor. "I always felt a little bit funny addressing him as Bill," he told me, "and he addressing me as Mr Tenney or Dr Tenney."

Watterson ended up drawing a number of sketches inspired by, and of, Mark Twain. Perfectly skewering the satirist's look with furrowed eyebrows and a hawked nose that plunges into the bushy moustache, Watterson left his indelible mark on part of Twain's legacy. Tenney used the images to make postcards to promote the journal, which he still offers to interested readers. "He was glad to make a little bit of money freelancing and I was glad to get the postcards," Tenney remembers fondly.

One of at least ten sketches that Watterson created is of particular interest in the story of *Calvin and Hobbes*. The cartoon accompanies an article entitled, "Tom Sawyer's Gang as Social Ritual: Implications for Modern Social Organization," and depicts a group of kids sitting around a boardroom table. An older twentysomething is lecturing five youngsters, while pointing at a graph that shows the "Projected Robberies and Murders" rate going upwards. At the far-left end of the table sits a small figure, a mop-topped kid with hair over his eyes, a striped shirt under a black sweatshirt. Like the little boy standing next to the fountain in his editorial cartoon for the *Cincinnati Post*, this is clearly an early version of Calvin. This same figure appears again at least four times in the *Sun Herald* in 1982, proving that Watterson was intrigued with this small figure and he wanted to flesh him out. Each time he drew him was confirmation for Watterson that he was on to something.

West himself gave Watterson an opportunity to contribute to a now legendary quarterly newsletter about the history of cartooning called *The Puck Papers*, which morphed into *Target* magazine in 1981. As well as writing opinion pieces and reviews, Watterson drew the very first cover for the venture, and five others, including those featuring gonzo artist extraordinaire Ralph Steadman, longstanding *Washington Post* editorial cartoonist Herblock and even one of West. "He enjoys making me look ridiculous," West jokes. "The cover wasn't my idea; he was just having fun at my expense."

During this period, Jim Borgman referred to Watterson as the "greatest unknown cartoonist in America," the kind of well-meaning compliment that may hurt more than it helps. He wasn't entirely unknown, because he had been making progressively bigger waves in Ohio, since he started in high school. He started to build up a public record of his art, though most of it was available to only a fraction of the audience that would later wholeheartedly embrace *Calvin and Hobbes*. Watterson clearly wanted to succeed at his long-time love of cartooning and he was going through great lengths to make this happen. If he could have seen what was around the corner, he might not have tried so hard.

CHAPTER 2

Making Friends

Calvin and Hobbes is genuine. It doesn't seem manufactured; it's very, very lifelike. The way Watterson made his characters move was genius. They're flesh and bone, and they're subject to gravity, wind, balance and all the forces of nature and physics. His characters don't look like inflated Macy's Day parade floats; they're real characters.

— Jef Mallett, creator of *Frazz*

In the aftermath of his unfortunate departure from the *Post* — and while he worked simultaneously as a layout artist, an editorial cartoonist and a freelance artist — Watterson pursued his true passion: comic strips. Whenever he had a spare moment, Watterson worked on ideas for a strip. It wasn't easy, because a sellable strip has to have all the right ingredients: great characters, good stories, funny punch lines and memorable artwork. Finding the perfect combination of these attributes is incredibly difficult and stymies many budding cartoonists before their creations even leave their bedrooms, basements and attics. And that's just the beginning.

After the artist has created a strip they are happy with, they must then produce a sample package of strips to send out to the syndicates, which poses a whole new set of hurdles. Trying to get a syndicate to consider representing your cartoon is a colossal effort akin to bands sending record companies their demos addressed to simply "A&R." In other words, the chances are slender that your work will be given measured consideration and even slimmer that someone might be interested in it.

The reality of the situation is that every year the syndicates are swamped by more strip submissions than they could hope to publish in the next millennia. Brendan Buford of King Features estimates that they get about 5,000 new comics a year. "A large percentage of them are absolutely horrible and worthless and can be dismissed after reading a couple of samples," he told me bluntly when I interviewed him to get a sense of the syndication process. "I am always behind on submissions, because there are those that deserve a great deal of attention. You very well may be staring at what could be the next big thing."

If a cartoonist is lucky enough to pique the interest of a syndicate, the syndicate will usually sign the artist to a development deal. This means the cartoonist gets a small fee to create a month or two of strips. Based on these samples, the syndicate will make suggestions on how to tweak it and get it ready for newspapers. This can some-times be a frustrating and time-consuming process, though anyone who makes it to that point will probably be published. "I don't ever sign a cartoonist to a development deal if I can't see their comic making it through to syndication," Buford told me. "It's a waste of time, a waste of money and a waste of resources."

Assuming the cartoonist makes it this far through the gauntlet, which may have taken a couple years, the syndicate then asks the artist to draw up a month's worth of strips and assigns the artist an editor. This usually takes a while, because all the cartoons submitted are unlikely to be publication-worthy. After much back and forth, refining and further development, a packet of solid work is finally assembled and the strip is ready to sell to newspapers. But the cartoonist shouldn't get too excited over the fact that the syndicate is repping the cartoonist's work, because that doesn't mean any newspapers are going to publish it. There is a very small, finite amount of space on the funny pages — and it's shrinking all the time — so comic strip real estate is very precious. The funny pages don't expand when there are a lot of good strips in the market, so when somebody gets a spot, it means that someone else just lost one. That being said, every cartoonist I spoke to for this book was generous and graceful when they spoke about losing a slot to a competitor. Many of them saw it as a challenge — only the strong cartoonists survive, so you'd better bring your A-game every day.

So, finally, assuming further that all goes as hoped, our cartoonist gets published in a few papers. When cartoonists are just starting out, they get a miniscule guarantee from their syndicate of probably only a few hundred dollars a week. After the syndicate breaks even on that guarantee, ensuing profits are split 50-50 between the artist and the syndicate. Cartoonists on the low end of the scale make $25,000 or less per year, leaving many up-and-coming comic strippers in need of freelance work or a second job to make ends meet. In contrast, heavyweights like Jim Davis, Garry Trudeau and Scott Adams can make hundreds of thousands of dollars a year just by syndicating their strips, and these estimated earnings don't even begin to take into account their income from books, merchandise and licensing. But for the most part, cartooning is not a get-rich-quick scheme, much like writing.

This was the dog-eat-dog world Watterson wanted to jump into without a bulletproof vest or parachute. By all accounts, he was fully aware that it wasn't a particularly easy road to take and that the rewards weren't usually high, or even assured. However, the grim odds of success didn't dissuade him and he plunged into the process of creating a comic strip with an admirable persistence.

Unfortunately, his first attempt at hitting the cartoonist's bull's eye was wide of the mark, though he would later fold a version of the failed strip's main character into *Calvin and Hobbes*. It was based on his German-class comic strip hero, Raumfahrer Rolf (Spaceman Rolf), who had morphed into the character Spaceman Mort in college, though Watterson never published any strips featuring that character. The latest incarnation, *Spaceman Spiff*, followed a blustering interstellar adventurer and his dull-witted assistant, Fargle.

A sarcastic send-up of classic sci-fi strips, *Spiff* paid backhanded homage to flashy space heroes like Buck Rogers and Flash Gordon, while tapping into the *Star Wars* craze. However, he was a far cry from the Spiff newspaper readers would come to love. "He was a more corrosive character," West remembers. "He smoked a stogie and was a midget. Part of the charm of Spaceman Spiff in *Calvin and Hobbes* was knowing that it was Calvin pretending to be Spaceman Spiff. In the strip *Spaceman Spiff*, there was no fantasy world."

Mike Keefe, an editorial cartoonist for the *Denver Post* from 1975 onwards, exchanged a few letters with Watterson after Watterson reviewed a collection of his, *Keefe-Kebab*, in *Target*. Watterson sent Keefe some examples of the *Spaceman Spiff* strip, hoping to get some constructive feedback. At that time, Keefe was doing a strip called *Iota* with Tim Menees through Universal Press Syndicate. Their editor was Lee Salem, who seemed to have a good grasp of what did and didn't work in the marketplace. So Keefe brought up the concept of the strip with Salem, who told him that he didn't feel that space strips were particularly marketable. This combination of adventure strip with over-the-top parody didn't sit well with any of the syndicates that Watterson approached and it was roundly rejected everywhere he sent it.

According to a 1986 interview with the *Plain Dealer*, around this time Watterson also tried a strip about a young newspaper reporter and his crazy editor, which was inspired by his time at the *Cincinnati Post*. And there was a *Pogo*-esque strip with a groundhog and a frog who lived in the woods. Neither got any interest from the syndicates. "I tried everything," Watterson admitted to the *Plain Dealer*. "Looking back on these [strips] is really embarrassing. I'm glad nobody can see them." He also tried developing another strip called *Critters*, which centered on small bug-like creatures, as well as another about a young person's first job and apartment. These, too, were flops with the syndicates. Years later, Watterson published a single panel from *Critters* in one of his collections, but none of these other early strips ever made their way into the public domain.

Though this deluge of rejection may have deterred meeker souls, Watterson kept plugging away. After these initial stumbles, he created *In The Dog House*, which he sent out to syndicates in March 1982. It starred a twentysomething named Sam — the Everyman — and his friend, Fester, who was essentially the slacker-loser from Watterson's college effort, *Mewkis and Fester*. Of most interest is Sam's little brother, named Marvin, who has a stuffed — perhaps live — tiger named Hobbes. Sound semi-familiar?

This was the first glimpse of the duo that would end up becoming Calvin and Hobbes. Though everyone ended up rejecting the strip,

United Features Syndicate said they were interested in looking at future work by the aspiring cartoonist, because of the promise *In the Dog House* showed. Watterson also received some positive feedback about the strip from some peers. He had been quietly sending his work out to established cartoonists whom he admired, including Berke Breathed, who was making waves with *Bloom County*. "I remember thinking, "Hey! This isn't the normal dreck; this looks pretty good,"" Breathed told me good-naturedly when I tracked him down. (More on that later.) "I'm hoping that I wrote him back a rare and very uncharacteristically positive response, because I'm usually very blunt with people. Usually I write, "I don't know this business — and I don't know what people want to read — but you can't even print and the drawing is awful." But his work caught my eye."

Rich West was friends with renowned editorial cartoonist Patrick Oliphant and offered to pass along Watterson's work to him. Oliphant had won the Pulitzer Prize for his political cartooning and Watterson was suitably in awe of his considerable talent. I found Oliphant, living in Santa Fe, still drawing and full of fond remembrances of Watterson's *In The Dog House*. "I thought it was a marvelous thing," Oliphant told me with a laid-back Australian drawl. "It became a lot more sophisticated as it went along, but it always had all the makings of being a great strip." He added, "I've seen Watterson's editorial cartoons and I'm glad he went on to do a comic strip instead."

One of the main criticisms *In The Dog House* got from everyone, including Oliphant, was that the strip seemed crowded. Taking this advice for what it was, Watterson began stripping away characters until he was left with only Sam, Fester, Marvin and Hobbes, and an early version of Susie Derkins. Marvin and Hobbes were fine-tuned further, but they were far from fully formed. "Marvin/Calvin was basically a wisecracker and his character wasn't much more developed than Garfield," West revealed to me. "There wasn't humanity in the early Calvin, but there was some magic in Bill's choice of making Hobbes come alive in that child's world — whereas he appeared to be a stuffed animal to everyone else. It was in that strip that Bill saw the potential of never-ending debate of whether Hobbes is real or not."

Watterson called the latest version *Fernbusterville* — a reference to his *Collegian* column *Pee Wee Fernbuster* — and sent it back to United Features, where it ended up on the desk of Sarah Gillespie, then the vice-president and director of comic art at the syndicate. Now retired, Gillespie lives on the Hudson line, north of New York City. Though she hasn't worked in the business for several years, she has clear memories of the times when she did. "We used to see 2,000 submissions a year," she remembered as we talked on the phone. "But Watterson's work stood out. Obviously, he had great potential." After corresponding for several months after his submission, Watterson flew out to meet Gillespie, who remembers him as a shy guy. "I don't think he ever called me Sarah," Gillespie recalls. "He was young enough that he used honorifics. He was incredibly polite, a nice kid. He had this Midwestern, nice-guy vibe."

Despite seeing real promise in Watterson's *Fernbusterville*, Gillespie still felt it missed the mark. She discerningly noted that the little kid, Marvin, and his tiger, Hobbes, were the true stars of the strip and it should revolve around their adventures. "*Fernbusterville* was a culmination of his genius, rather a collapse of his genius," West says in retrospect. "He was trying so hard to listen to all the advice that he just threw everything and the kitchen sink into this danged strip. And it was too much and lacked focus."

Though he felt his work kept getting better and he was growing as an artist, Watterson was a working definition of a pessimist during this period, as Rich West remembers. "He was increasingly doubtful that something would happen. Each rejection was a confirmation of his pessimism. The syndicates present a fortress-like façade to young cartoonists. Though they can be courteous, it's rare that they are encouraging, or enthusiastic. They're not there to coddle up-and-coming cartoonists, and they certainly didn't coddle Bill. One of his greatest frustrations, though, was the extraordinary length of time when there was no communication between him and the syndicates. Bill was reluctant to press the matter, because no answer was better than a negative answer at that time in his career. But it wasn't a fun time."

"He got rejected so much it was discouraging," Bill's father told the *Cleveland Plain Dealer* in 1987. "We'd look at what was coming back and knew it was so much better than what we were seeing in the papers. We kept thinking, Why doesn't somebody else recognize this?" However, Watterson told the *Houston Chronicle* that he came to understand these early rejections. "In all of [my early strips], I can see flaws."

In the introduction to *The Complete Calvin and Hobbes* many years later, Watterson was equally pragmatic assessing his rejections: "I'm honestly grateful that all my early strip submissions were flatly rejected," he declared. "This was not a case of syndicate editors failing to recognize latent genius. My strips had serious flaws, so I'm very lucky I didn't get stuck trying to make one of them fly."

He knew that to create a successful strip, he would have to concoct characters and a premise that could ultimately "write themselves" and not become stale within a few months. Unfortunately, the efforts from this era didn't fit those criteria. "My early strip proposals were unevenly written," Watterson admitted in *The Complete Calvin and Hobbes*. "[They had] an occasional good character surrounded by flat ones, put into limited or clichéd worlds beyond my experience. These are common mistakes, but the only way to learn how to write and draw is by writing and drawing. The good thing about working with almost no audience was that I felt free to experiment. Nobody cared what I did, so I tried pretty much anything that came into my head, acquired some new skills along the way, and gradually learned a bit about what worked and what didn't."

Watterson talked about the evolution of his strips years later to *Honk!*: "It was a slow process," he admitted. He was, at first, very tentative about concentrating just on Calvin and Hobbes. "I was afraid that maybe the key to their wackiness was the contrast between them and the more normal characters in the rest of the strip," he continued. "I wasn't sure Calvin and Hobbes would be able to maintain that intensity on their own. But I tried it, and almost immediately it clicked in my mind; it became much easier to write material. Their personalities expanded easily, and that takes a good seventy-five percent of the work out of it. If you have the personalities down, you understand them and identify with them; you can stick them in any situation and have a pretty good idea of how they're going to respond. Then it's just a matter of sanding and polishing up the jokes. But if you've got more ambiguous characters or stock stereotypes, the plastic comes through and they don't work as well. These two characters clicked for me almost immediately and I feel very comfortable working with them."

"Bill's never been arrogant about his abilities," West revealed.

"But he had some confidence that if he was given the chance he could create something interesting. He knew what he didn't like, and he knew what he liked, and he was ready to work hard to try to make something special." And work he did. Based on United's feedback, he scaled back the strip yet again and concentrated on the kid Marvin and his tiger. Marvin's name was changed to Calvin in July 1983, because Tom Armstrong's strip *Marvin* had launched the previous year, and Watterson didn't want there to be any confusion.

He later told an interviewer in 1987 that the names Calvin and Hobbes were "a tip of the hat to the political science department at Kenyon College . . . I thought it was funny." Calvin was named after the sixteenth-century Protestant theologian who believed in predestination, Hobbes after the philosopher a century later who once observed that life is "nasty, brutish and short." Or that's what Watterson would have you believe. "That's not true," Rich West told me. "The linking of the two names wasn't natural. The strip did not come from the idea that both characters would be named after philosophical thinkers. However, Hobbes was definitely a tip of the hat — and perhaps a little bit of a smirk at — his political science degree from Kenyon. Calvin was just a coincidence."

So for the first time the strip concentrated on a boy named Calvin and his doll/tiger named Hobbes. Physically, Calvin looked the same as readers came to know him — all torso with shorts legs — but in this early version of the strip he had a Beatles-esque mop-top haircut that covered his eyes, something that would seem so jarring to fans now. "Bill realized he was losing an extraordinary opportunity for comic expression," West recounts now. So Watterson gave Calvin a haircut in July 1985, just when the sales packet for *Calvin and Hobbes* was being prepared.

This was a pivotal moment in Watterson's life. He had created the pair of anti-heroes: a mischievous six-year-old and his constant companion, a tiger named Hobbes (who may or may not be real). The simple conceit of the strip — Calvin sees one thing and the adults something else entirely — is a revolutionary idea. Subjective reality had come into play before, but this is the first time it was so concisely expressed in a comic strip. In these flights of fancy lies the genius of *Calvin*. The characters in the strip view the world through two different lenses, each one giving insight into a different reality. There was the one Calvin and Hobbes peered through and the one the other characters looked through. Though Calvin saw Hobbes as a tiger and went on all sorts of fantastical adventures with him, everyone else just saw a boy playing ridiculous games with his doll. "The so-called "gimmick" of my strip — the two versions of Hobbes — is sometimes misunderstood," Watterson clarified in his essay for the *Tenth Anniversary* collection. "I don't think of Hobbes as a doll that miraculously comes to life when Calvin's around. Neither do I think of Hobbes as the product of Calvin's imagination. Calvin sees Hobbes one way, and everyone else sees Hobbes another way. I show two versions of reality, and each makes complete sense to the participant who sees it."

Watterson discussed this conceit with *Honk!* in 1987. "I hate to subject it to too much analysis," he continued. "One thing I have fun with is the rarity of things being shown from an adult's perspective. When Hobbes is a stuffed toy in one panel and alive in the next, I'm juxtaposing the "grown-up" version of reality with Calvin's version, and inviting the reader to decide which is truer." Most of the time, Watterson drew the strip from Calvin's perspective, so Hobbes was alive, and he didn't want to keep reminding readers that Hobbes was a stuffed animal to the other characters. "I try to get the reader completely swept up into Calvin's world by ignoring adult perspective," he professed in the *Honk!* interview. "Hobbes, therefore, isn't just a cute gimmick. I'm not making the strip revolve around the transformation. The viewpoint of the strip fluctuates, and this allows Hobbes to be a "real" character."

I remember understanding this conceit immediately as a young reader, because having a dual reality is one of the best parts of being a kid. There's your world and then there's the grown-ups' world. The boring adult world doesn't have a tribe of hostile Indians hiding behind the front hedge or a giant albino panda that's lurking in the woods behind the house. As a result, the adults could never understand why a child (in this case, me) would have to run off with a laser gun to save his entire family from impending doom and unacceptable mayhem.

Watterson later admitted to *The Comics Journal* in 1989 that he didn't think the conceit of his strip was that groundbreaking. "It's a strip about a family — a familiar, universal setting that's easy to identify with," he said. "I'm trying to put a unique twist on it, but it's well-covered ground . . . Still, with any strip, it's not the subject that's important, it's what you do with it. A family strip can be hackneyed drivel just as easily as any other kind of strip."

Watterson wrote about the inspiration for Calvin in *The Calvin and Hobbes Tenth Anniversary Book*. "Most people assume that Calvin is based on a son of mine, or based on detailed memories of my own childhood. In fact, I don't have children, and I was a fairly quiet, obedient kid — almost Calvin's opposite. One of the reasons that Calvin's character is fun to write is that I often don't agree with him."

Over the course of his public commentaries and dissections on Calvin, Watterson could never seem to decide how much of Calvin was in him ". . . Calvin is autobiographical in the sense that he thinks about the same issues that I do," Watterson wrote in an essay for *The Calvin and Hobbes Tenth Anniversary Book.* "[I]n this, Calvin reflects my own adulthood more than my childhood. Many of Calvin's struggles are metaphors for my own. I suspect that most of us get old without growing up, and that inside every adult (sometimes not very far inside) is a bratty kid who wants everything his way. I use Calvin as an outlet for my immaturity, as a way to keep myself curious about the natural world, as a way to ridicule my obsessions, and as a way to comment on human nature. I wouldn't want Calvin in my house, but on paper, he helps me sort through my life and understand it." He continued this self-analysis of Calvin with *Honk!*: "Calvin [is] more energetic, brash, always looking for life on the edge," he acknowledged. "He lives entirely in the present, and whatever he can do to make that moment more exciting he'll just let fly . . . and I'm really not like that at all."

However, he later admitted in *The Calvin and Hobbes Tenth Anniversary Book* that the "fictional and non-fictional aspects were pretty densely interwoven. While Calvin definitely reflects certain aspects of my personality, I never had imaginary animal friends, I generally stayed out of trouble, I did fairly well in school . . . so the strip is not literally autobiographical." "I tried not to use my life that directly," he continued later, in an interview with fans to celebrate the release of *The Complete Calvin and Hobbes.* "Whenever I started to cross that line, it felt exploitive. Real-life issues gave me a subject to work with, but then I made up the stories. Inconvenient facts were deleted, details were moved around, and wholly fictitious parts were added, all to fit the needs of the strip. My family certainly recognized the context of a lot of strips, but I tried to keep the true parts as just the starting point."

Hobbes was in part inspired by Watterson's gray tabby, Sprite, who served as a model for the tiger's personality and movements. "She was good-natured, intelligent, friendly, and enthusiastic in a sneaking-up-and-pouncing sort of way," Watterson later wrote in *The Calvin and Hobbes Tenth Anniversary Book*. The cat also gave Watterson the idea for Hobbes's leaping ambushes of Calvin at the door. However, the artist usually demurred in interviews from giving too much insight into his feline star. "Hobbes is really hard to define and, in a way, I'm reluctant to do it," Watterson told *The Comics Journal*. "[T]here's something a little peculiar about him that's, hopefully, not readily categorized."

"Hobbes is more of a subtle character and it took me a little longer to get a bead on him," Watterson told the *Plain Dealer* in 1987. "Animal characters in general tend to get more attention," he says. "You can almost hang yourself with it. Almost as soon as you put an animal in the strip they take over. *Bloom County*, for example, really took off when Opus came. There's always some danger of the character running away with the strip. In *Peanuts*, Snoopy has taken the lead role. You have to watch that kind of thing. Just make sure the animal isn't changing the strip in a direction you don't want to go in."

Watterson's wife, Melissa, provided some of the basis for Calvin's crush-turned-nemesis, Susie Derkins ("Derkins" was even the name of Melissa's family's beagle). "Susie is earnest, serious, and smart — the kind of girl I was attracted to in high school and eventually married," Watterson wrote in the introductory essay to the *Tenth*

Anniversary collection. "I suspect Calvin has a mild crush on her that he expresses by trying to annoy her, but Susie is a bit unnerved and put off by Calvin's weirdness. This encourages Calvin to be even weirder, so it's a good dynamic. Neither of them quite understands what's going on, which is probably true of most relationships."

With a head-hugging bowl cut that looks as if it's for a Lego mini-figure, and a penchant for overalls, Susie plays lacrosse and has a mean pitching arm. Despite this tomboy streak, she still spends a lot of time throwing tea parties for her dolls. Like Calvin, she carries around her own stuffed animal — a rabbit named Mr Bun — but there's never any evidence that their relationship works the same way that Calvin and Hobbes's does. In one strip, she brings over Mr Bun to play with the pair, prompting Calvin to demand, "Hobbes and I are gonna put our big plans on hold so we can play house with a stuffed rabbit?" In the last frame, Hobbes notes, "Mr Bun seems comatose," perhaps wondering why the rabbit doesn't get up and join in the way he does.

When it came to Calvin's parents, Watterson borrowed inspiration from his own life. Like Calvin's father, Watterson's father was also a patent attorney who loved to cycle. Slender, with dark hair and glasses, he looks not unlike the few photos of Watterson's father that I came across during my research. My hunch was right, I soon discovered. "Calvin's dad is . . . a satire of my own father," Watterson admitted in the *Tenth Anniversary* essay. "Any strip about how suffering "builds character" is usually verbatim transcripts for why we were all freezing, exhausted, hungry, and lost on camping trips. These things are a lot funnier after twenty-five years have passed." Watterson singled out one strip in particular in *The Calvin and Hobbes Tenth Anniversary Book* — "This is my dad. No exaggeration" — in which the father comes in after a brisk morning workout. "Ahh, what a day," he exclaims, with ruddy cheeks and clothing covered in snow. "Up at 6:00, a 10-mile run in the sleet, and now a big bowl of plain oatmeal! How I love the crazy hedonism of the weekends!"

According to everyone I spoke with, Calvin's mother doesn't draw inspiration from Watterson's mother. This is probably a good thing, because readers may develop a certain amount of pity for her, especially at mealtimes. She clearly works hard to have nice lunches and dinners ready, but Calvin doesn't appreciate any of this hard work and sometimes her husband is just as ungrateful. The only times Calvin gets excited is when he believes the meal is actually something disgusting, like spider pie or monkey heads. For the most part, Calvin's mother is either disciplining him, cleaning up after him or trying to get him to the bus on time. You rarely see her relaxing and, if you do, it's usually the moment before Calvin breaks her reverie with some prank.

Despite the fact that Calvin's parents purposely didn't have names, Watterson wanted to insure they weren't stereotypes fulfilling their roles blankly. "I don't want the parents to simply function as parents," Watterson emphasized to *The Comics Journal* years later. "I want them to be unique individuals as well. They are parents, of course, and, as sane people, they have to react to Calvin's personality. What I try to do in writing any character is to put myself in his position, to the extent that I can, and I know that if I was Calvin's dad or Calvin's mom that I would not react to him with the gooey sentimentality that sometimes appears in other strips. Given Calvin's usual behavior, I think his parents show admirable restraint in theirs."

So here they were: Calvin, Hobbes, his parents and Susie. This was the cast Watterson wanted to form the backbone of his latest iteration. When he resubmitted his strip with the re-envisioned cast, now called *Calvin and Hobbes*, to United Features Syndicate in late summer of 1983, it hit the nail on the head for Sarah Gillespie. She offered him a development deal almost immediately. "The deal was done so we could hold on to the strip," she admits now. "It would keep him submitting material, so we could keep seeing what he was up to. And what he was up to was wonderful and very impressive." Watterson was given around $1,000 as a retainer and asked to draw up a month of cartoons for Sarah and her United co-workers.

Even then, Gillespie knew that she was dealing with a breakout strip. "I wouldn't be so egotistical as to say I knew it was something great," she says now. "But I certainly knew it was something special and that someone would pick it up and he would have a good shot at success. It wasn't the only comic I ever saw where I said "This is wonderful," but I certainly thought he had a good shot [at] being the next Schulz."

Dave Hendin, then senior vice-president and editorial director at United, remembers first reading the strip when Gillespie brought it to the senior group's attention. Like Gillespie, he is now retired, living outside New York and easy enough to find with a little digging around. When I caught up with him, he was happy to remember his small role in the history of *Calvin and Hobbes*. Hendin was a part of the editorial group at United who met every few weeks to check out the new submissions and pass around the latest projects. "*Calvin and Hobbes* had very favorable feedback," Hendin remembered. "It was a damn good strip from the beginning and a number of us liked it very much. I can't tell you how many comic strips I've seen that looked great for the first two months, but the creator could neither sustain it nor build on it. Bill had the kind of genius where he was able to do both."

Hendin and Gillespie were under a great deal of pressure from the corporate executives of United's parent company, the media giant Scripps, to bring in higher profits. At the time, United was representing both *Peanuts* and *Garfield*, which were big earners for the company. "So, the people at the parent company were seeing this big money coming in and were saying "Why don't you do make these other strips as popular as *Peanuts* and *Garfield* and then we can all make a lot more money?"" Hendin related to me. "Unfortunately, that's not the way it works. You can't spend money to make a great comic strip; you have to find the right person to make a great comic strip."

To determine which strips had the most commercial potential, Scripps insisted United use focus groups for their untested comic strips. Doing as they were told, the United team took several strips to the focus groups, including *Calvin and Hobbes*. Perhaps *Drabble* and *Rose is Rose* were presented, but neither Hendin nor Gillespie can remember for sure. There were between three and five separate tests, during which focus groups rated the strips and debated their pros and cons. Then all the strips were scored and ranked according to the feedback.

Unfortunately, and quite surprisingly, *Calvin and Hobbes* tested poorly. As Gillespie puts it, with a touch of understandable bitterness, "United didn't take *Calvin and Hobbes* because a couple housewives in Connecticut said, "It's okay, but we don't get it.""Gillespie got angry with the results and went to her boss to complain. She told him that if United didn't take *Calvin and Hobbes*, someone else would. "Fuck it, we can't take everything," she was told. Hendin tried his own "Hail Mary" with their boss, but his plea fell on deaf ears. "It was one of those things," Hendin says now with pragmatism. "Everybody but United rejected *Peanuts*. Everybody rejected *Garfield*. To miss something really good is nothing to be ashamed of in a creative environment. If you recognize that, you have a chance to get the next one."

Gillespie doesn't subscribe to that school of thought. "I took our loss of *Calvin and Hobbes* pretty personally," she freely admits now. "That may have been why I needed to get out of the business. As an editor you're not the creative person, but if you're a good editor and you've got a good nose for it, then you can fight for the good stuff. I fought for it, but I'll never know if I fought hard enough. It was a true professional disappointment."

Despite the fact that upper management didn't believe in *Calvin and Hobbes*, everyone agreed that Watterson was a fine artist whose skills could be put to other uses. The marketing department had obtained the rights to a character named Robotman and they wanted someone to create a comic strip around the character, so they could use the strip as a springboard to merchandising and animating opportunities. Overriding advice from Gillespie and others at United, executives insisted she offer the opportunity to Watterson.

Gillespie was uncomfortable and hesitant about doing it, but she nonetheless flew Watterson to New York City in January 1984 to discuss incorporating the Robotman character into *Calvin and Hobbes*. "I didn't like the idea of having a comic forced upon somebody," she says now. "I was embarrassed by the entire thing." Gillespie's assessment of the situation was astute and Watterson balked. "They thought that maybe I could stick [Robotman] in my strip, working with Calvin's imagination or something," Watterson told *Honk!* in 1987. "They didn't really care too much how I did it, just so long as the character remained intact and would be a very major character."

Watterson declined the offer politely, but firmly. "My impression was that it was never really considered," Gillespie says now. "I felt badly about bringing him in, because I felt it was disrespectful. It really went against my idea of what a comic strip should be," Watterson confessed to *Honk!* years later. "I'm not interested in slamming United Features here. Keep in mind that, at the time, it was the only syndicate that had expressed any interest in my work. I remain grateful for their early attention . . . Not knowing if *Calvin and Hobbes* would ever go anywhere, it was difficult to turn down another chance at syndication. But I really recoiled at the idea of drawing somebody else's character. It's cartooning by committee, and I have a moral problem with that. It's not art then."

After Watterson turned her down, Gillespie offered *Robotman* to up-and-comer Jim Meddick. Meddick had won a contest for his own strip *Paperback Writer* while he was still in college. When he graduated, he started submitting it to a number of syndicates, including United. They expressed an interest, but wanted him to sign a development contract that he felt was too one-sided, so he turned it down. Consequently, he was offered *Robotman*, which he took on with a pragmatic air. "It wasn't my character, so I wasn't worried about losing it," he admitted when I caught up with him. "To be honest, I didn't think they would even launch it. I thought that since it was designed to be a toy for children it wouldn't work as a comic strip. However, they were offering me cash to work on it, so I figured I would get some money and learn how to draw a strip at the same time. No matter what, it was win-win for me."

Though Gillespie didn't think the strip was the right fit for Watterson, she didn't necessarily feel the same about *Robotman* and Meddick, and has since been impressed with Meddick's work. "There were times I would look at him and I would feel badly about kind of sticking this on him, but the fact that Meddick made it into something worthwhile is really a testament to his talent." *Robotman* launched in 1985 and though it never became the licensing juggernaut the marketing department had hoped, it nonetheless became a hit in its own right. Over the years, Meddick added his own characters to the strip, including a geeky inventor named Monty Montahue, who would go on to become the star and namesake of the strip. Today *Monty* still runs in papers and online, a surprising outcome to an odd little sidebar story.

Despite United's crushing rejection, Watterson was confident that he was on to something with *Calvin and Hobbes* and decided to send his work to other syndicates to see if they might bite. In February 1984, he submitted it to the Washington Post Syndicate, but they weren't interested. Later that year, in November, he sent it to Universal Press Syndicate. Since there were only a finite number of syndicates, this submission was something of a last-ditch effort, but it was a gamble that paid off in spades.

Then editor Lee Salem of the Universal Press Syndicate still remembers seeing Watterson's first submissions. "I loved it. It was just a breath of fresh air. I was so impressed by the work that I had to set it aside, just so I could look at it later and see if my initial reaction was warranted." Salem even used his own focus group on the strips to double-check himself. "I took them home to my kids," he told me. "My son was about nine and my daughter was about 11 and they both fell in love immediately. My son had the great line, "This is *Doonesbury* for kids," which I actually used at the presentation of the comics to our sales team." Salem was sold.

Salem still works at Universal to this day, where he's now the president of the syndicate. His memories of *Calvin and Hobbes* hang on the walls near his desk in the form of several strips that Watterson gave him over the years. He's an affable guy on the phone, quickly likable, without being ingratiating. He was kind enough to speak with me on several occasions, standing in for his absent cartoonist.

In March 1985, Salem and UPS flew Watterson to Kansas City to offer him a contract. But before he could sign it, he had to officially extricate himself from his development deal with United, which meant giving them back the thousand-dollar retainer. "It was embarrassing," says Gillespie. "I never asked for it, but he sent it to me, along with a letter. It was very nice and I felt terrible about it, mostly because I knew he was going to be successful."

Free of any obligations to United, Watterson signed with Universal Press Syndicate in the spring of 1985 and immediately began writing and drawing at a furious pace. He had been stumbling around in the wilderness for years, and now he was finally where he wanted to be. He had gone down some wrong roads, but all indications told him that this was the path he was meant to be on.

CHAPTER 3

Standing on the Shoulders of Giants

A lot of people rip on Dylan's voice or the harmonica, but I always say, "Whatever you think about his music, the road runs through him. You have to come to terms with him, whether you want to or not." It's the same with Watterson. I don't know anyone who doesn't like *Calvin and Hobbes*, but if I did meet someone like that, I'd just tell them that the road runs through Watterson.

— Stephan Pastis, creator of *Pearls Before Swine*

Without Shakespeare there wouldn't have been *10 Things I Hate About You*. Without *The Godfather* there would be no *Sopranos*. And without the Beatles there would be no Oasis, Tears for Fears would never have written "Sowing The Seeds of Love" and I wouldn't own all those dodgy Paul McCartney solo albums. No matter how singular someone's genius is, that person inevitably stands on the shoulders of giants. Watterson is no different and many characters, cartoonists and artists paved the way for him. Though he complimented a number of strips when given the chance, he always mentioned three in particular as having a sizable impact on his craft: Walt Kelly's *Pogo*, George Herriman's *Krazy Kat* and Charles Schulz's *Peanuts*.

Many younger readers of this book who have not delved far into the wild and wonderful world of American cartooning will only be familiar with *Peanuts*, which for a long time was the most widely read comic strip in the world. *Peanuts* is often credited by cartoonists as being the ultimate strip; certainly the strip that set the bar for modern cartooning. "Charles M. Schulz is in a league all his own," Watterson wrote in an essay for the *Los Angeles Times* in 1999. "He was a hero to me as a kid and his influence on my work and life is long and deep. I suspect most cartoonists would say something similar." Watterson told *Honk!* magazine in 1987 that his respect for the comic continued well into adulthood. "Every now and then I hear that *Peanuts* isn't as funny as it was or it's gotten old or something like that," he noted. "I think what's really happened is that Schulz, in *Peanuts*, changed the entire face of comic strips, and everybody has now caught up to him."

Watterson heaped praise on his childhood hero whenever he got the chance. In his *Los Angeles Times* piece he explained what he enjoyed about the artistry of *Peanuts*. "Graphically, the strip is static and spare," he admitted. "Schulz gave up virtually all the "cinematic" devices that create visual drama: there are no fancy perspectives, no interesting croppings, no shadows and lighting effects, no three-dimensional modeling, few props and few settings. Schulz distilled each subject to its barest essence, and drew it straight on or in side view, in simple outlines. But while the simplicity of Schulz's drawings made the strip stand out from the rest, it was the expressiveness within the simplicity that made Schulz's artwork so forceful."

Peanuts follows Charlie Brown and his cast of neighborhood friends, including his imaginative beagle Snoopy, wunderkind pianist Schroeder, blanket-loving Linus, bossy Lucy and tomboy Peppermint Patty, amongst others. It often focuses on Charlie Brown's never-ending failures, whether it's his ineffectual pining for the semi-mythical "red-haired girl" or his inability to ever kick the football that Lucy holds for him, but it always tries to put a funny spin on these defeatist moments.

Schulz's real mark as a cartoonist was his ability to keep his readers interested in the foibles of his kid creations for nearly 50 years. Interestingly, Schulz wrote, drew, lettered and inked every strip and so did Watterson. Artistically, the two men overlapped on occasion and it is easy to see where Watterson might have borrowed from the cartooning icon. The downpours that Calvin and his family were treated to on summer camping trips looked a lot like the rainstorms Schulz used to douse his characters with on the playing field. Both artists were able to perfectly capture the feeling of a wall of rain using fine straight slashes across entire panels. Another Schulz-ian flourish in Watterson's strips was the parentheses around Calvin's eyes when he felt apprehensive, which mirrored Charlie Brown when he would have one of his many anxious moments.

Both Calvin and Charlie tried playing baseball — and they both sucked. Unlike Charlie Brown though, Calvin doesn't want to excel at it, he just wants to be left to his own devices. The harder he tries to avoid playing the sport, the more it haunts him. The one time that Calvin's father takes him out to play baseball in the backyard, their practice ends abruptly when a bouncing grounder knocks out Calvin. At another juncture, the baseball tries to attack Calvin, and during a baseball game at school Calvin manages to catch out a teammate. There are other similarities between the boys. Both of them liked making snowmen (though Calvin's morbidly fantastical creations were a world away from anything that ever appeared in *Peanuts*) and each had a lovable pet that served as a companion and a psychologist.

Despite these similarities, Calvin was no Charlie Brown knock-off. Calvin may have been sarcastic and cynical, but he was never a chronic worrywart or manic-depressive like Charlie Brown. Charlie Brown would routinely say the most depressing things ever uttered. A perfect example of this can be found in the 19 November 1991 *Peanuts*: Charlie Brown, watching a dance program with Sally Brown, remarks, "I like to watch people having a good time," before adding, with a whiff of kill-me-now morbidity, "I've always wanted to have a good time."

Watterson recognized the dark side of Schulz in his piece for the *Los Angeles Times*: "Schulz reminds us that our fears and insecurities are not much different when we grow up . . . For a "kid strip" with "gentle humor," it shows a pretty dark world, and I think this is what makes the strip so different from, and so much more significant than, other comics. Only with the inspired surrealism of Snoopy does the strip soar into silliness and fantasy. And even then, the Red Baron shoots the doghouse full of holes."

Watterson and Schulz ended up corresponding in the late '80s and Watterson sent his hero a hand-colored Sunday strip, which to this day hangs in the hallway of Schulz's former studio. Schulz was even kind enough to write the introduction to *The Essential Calvin and Hobbes*. His short, but immensely warm, essay is fun and funny, relishing in the whimsy of Watterson's work. "Bill Watterson draws wonderful bedside tables," Schulz begins. "I admire that. He also draws great water splashes and living room couches and chairs and lamps and yawns and screams, and all the things that make a comic strip fun to look at. I like the thin little arms on Calvin and his shoes that look like dinner rolls."

The two men never ended up meeting face-to-face. "I cannot remember any particular conversations about Bill," Jeannie Schulz told me in a brief email exchange. "But I do know that if asked, Schulz was always complimentary." In interviews, Schulz professed that *Calvin and Hobbes* was one of the strips he read every day.

A lighter inspiration for Watterson was George Herriman's *Krazy Kat*, a strip populated by animals who spoke their own nonsensical patois and lived in Coconino County, Arizona. The strip starred the oddest of love triangles. There was Krazy Kat, who was in love with the mouse, Ignatz, who didn't return the adoration. Ignatz did love to throw rocks at Krazy Kat though, which Krazy Kat took as a sign of affection. And then there was Offisa Pup, who was in love with Krazy Kat, but he never made any progress because Krazy Kat was always mooning over Ignatz.

Sometimes silly and oftentimes nonsensical, *Krazy Kat* usually made you feel like there was a joke you were missing, which isn't necessarily a good thing when you're reading the funnies. Watterson talked about his love for Herriman when West interviewed him for *The Comics Journal*. "*Krazy Kat* is a completely unique strip," Watterson opined. "I think it's the best comic strip ever drawn. Ultimately, though, it's such a peculiar and idiosyncratic vision that it has little to say to me directly. I marvel at it because it's beyond duplication. It's like trying to paint a sunrise — you're better off not even trying."

"Those strips were just complete worlds that the reader would be sucked into," Watterson told *Honk!* magazine. "*Krazy Kat* . . . had tremendous dialogue and fantastic backgrounds. For a few moments a day we could live in Coconino County; the whole thing was entirely there. The dialogue was part of it, the backgrounds were part of it, the characters were offbeat . . . and you need a little space and time to develop that sort of thing. I know for a fact that nobody's doing it now and I don't know that anybody will do it." Watterson definitely learned from Herriman's backgrounds, which often featured a southwestern mesa reminiscent of the red planets that Spaceman Spiff would one day crash-land on. If you look closely enough at the *Calvin and Hobbes* Sunday strip from 17 May 1987, you'll find Calvin's parents looking at a painting in a museum. The artwork is actually a *Krazy Kat* landscape.

In 1990, Watterson wrote the foreword to *The Komplete Kolor Krazy Kat*, in which he expounded upon his love and respect for the strip. "As a cartoonist, I read *Krazy Kat* with awe and wonder," he wrote. "*Krazy Kat* is such a pure and completely realized personal vision that the strip's inner mechanism is ultimately as unknowable as George Herriman. Nevertheless, I marvel at how this fanciful world could be so forcefully imagined and brought to paper with such immediacy. THIS is how good a comic strip can be." He finishes with a flourish, "*Krazy Kat* is like no other comic strip before or after it. We are richer for Herriman's integrity and vision."

The third strip Watterson continually referenced as a major inspiration was *Pogo*. The strip followed talking animals living in Okefenokee Swamp that were as sarcastic as they were satirical, and as controversial as they were confrontational. Centering on the high jinks and commentary-filled adventures of Pogo the possum, Albert the alligator and a rotating cast of supporting characters that topped out at over 300, the strip was marketed to children and beloved by adults. Infused with radically liberal storylines that often didn't hold back their political potshots, the strips set a new bar for depth and intellect on the comics page.

Created by Walt Kelly in 1941, *Pogo* ultimately spawned animated films, action figures, even an LP of Kelly's verses set to music. Kelly had worked as a Disney animator for years and it is indubitable that his time in the Magic Kingdom influenced his own work. Though his animals would never be mistaken for Walt's creations, their animated quality on the page couldn't help but remind readers of classic talking animals like Dumbo and Bambi.

In a speech celebrating Walt Kelly's life and work given at Ohio State University in 1988, Watterson described the strip as one of his biggest influences, before going on to talk about how hard it was for him to track down the rare and out-of-print copies of Kelly's collections for his personal library. The treasure hunt to find these books spawned a series of nightmares for Watterson, which he psychoanalyzed good-naturedly. "I walk into a book store, and am astounded to find row after row of *Pogo* books that I'd never seen before," he disclosed, "twenty or thirty books that no one has heard of. Obviously, they would complete my collection. With typical dream perversity, I discover I have just five dollars in my wallet, enough to buy only one book. I know that if I run home to get more money, someone else will buy all the other books before I get back. So, with a horrible mixture of excitement and despair, I flip through the books trying to decide which one to get. I wake up clammy with sweat every time. And now I take a charge card everywhere I go."

In the same speech, Watterson discussed one of the lessons he learned from Kelly. "[I]f you can sum up who your characters are in a sentence or two, you're in trouble. People are complicated, and cartoon characters need to reflect that complexity to be intriguing to the reader. One reason *Pogo* is fun to read and reread is that the core characters are many-sided. They react differently in different circumstances. They all have good sides and bad that reveal themselves gradually. The characters are full of life and unpredictability." Watterson took a cue from Kelly's thoughtful and rich character development, carefully balancing the evolution of Calvin and Hobbes with their unfolding humanity over the course of their ten-year run.

The *Calvin and Hobbes* creator also took a cue from Kelly's self-penned poetry, which littered his *Pogo* books. Watterson employed this device when he had the space in Sunday strips or within his own collections. His playful poems oftentimes took the form of odes to Hobbes or secret songs for the GROSS (Get Rid Of Slimy girlS) club, though he didn't limit himself to those vehicles. *Yukon Ho!* opens with a poem-turned-lighthearted-battle-cry as Calvin and Hobbes set their sights on a brave new world: "The Yukon is the place for us! / That's where we want to live. / Up there we'll get to yell and cuss / And act real primitive." Their swaggering declaration of independence imagines a world where they wouldn't have to eat Mom's bad cooking or put up with "monstrous, crabby teachers." Just the kind of world that seems like paradise to a kid.

You could feel Watterson's love of the natural world in each brushstroke and pen line in *Yukon Ho!*, whether he was drawing a leafless poplar tree, a gurgling creek or a star-speckled night sky. So it was no surprise when Watterson took a pro-environmental stance, long before being green was vogue. In the 19 July 1987 strip, Calvin and Hobbes discover some discarded cans in the woods: "By golly, if people aren't burying toxic wastes or testing nuclear weapons, they're throwing trash everywhere," Calvin rants. "You'd think planets like this were dime a dozen!" Hobbes responds that it's at times like this that he's proud to not be human, which prompts Calvin to strip off his clothes in solidarity.

This strip in particular invokes Walt Kelly's similar indignation over the desecration of the environment. Watterson undoubtedly read Kelly's *We Have Met The Enemy and He Is Us*. This *Pogo* collection opens with a vicious essay from the cartoonist: "Humans . . . are generally two-legged, fumble-fingered slobs whose indolent wits enable them by and large to be sitting ducks," Kelly sneered. "The big polluter did not start out with smokestacks. He didn't start pumping gunk into the waters of our world when he was six years old. He started small. Throwing papers underfoot in the streets, heaving old bottles into vacant lots, leaving the remnants of a picnic in the fields and woodlands. Just like the rest of us."

Watterson was never as condemnatory as Kelly, but the environment is a subject that he clearly feels passionate about. Calvin brings up the Greenhouse Effect with his mother while she waters her flowers in the 23 July 1987 strip. "They say the pollutants we dump in the air are trapping in the sun's heat," Calvin exposits. "It's going to melt the polar ice caps! Sure, you'll be gone when it happens, but I won't! Nice planet you're leaving me." His mother turns and addresses the reader: "This from the kid who wants to be chauffeured any place more than a block away." Whether these eco-conscious strips were inspired by Kelly's forays into similar territory, we may never know.

Aside from these three heroes routinely championed by Watterson, there are undoubtedly other influences on his work. Winsor McCay's *Little Nemo in Slumberland*, a lushly drawn full page Sunday strip that ran at the turn of the twentieth century, was probably another touchstone for Watterson. The strip was almost psychedelic — like *Alice in Wonderland* rewritten by Edgar Rice Burroughs and Ken Kesey. McCay had used dream sequences in his early strip *The Dream of the Rarebit Fiend*, but expanded the concept in *Little Nemo*. In each episode, the boy Nemo goes off on a series of fantastical adventures, only to be awakened at the end of them by falling out of bed. To drive the point home with an even heavier hand, he would usually say something like, "Oh! Where am I? Huh! I was only dreaming!"

Watterson wrote a piece for *The Best of Little Nemo* in 1997. "*Little Nemo*'s dream imagery . . . is as mind-bending today as ever," Watterson declared. "And Winsor McCay remains one of the greatest innovators and manipulators of the comic strip medium. Nobody did fantasy like this before, and very few have tried it since." *Little Nemo in Slumberland* was never hugely popular during its three separate runs, but it has undergone a renaissance in the last 20 years. Recently, a gorgeous — and gigantic — collection entitled *Splendid Sundays* was released, featuring 120 restored, full-size strips, which is a must-have for anyone unfamiliar with the strip or who would like to delve into Calvin's lineage further.

"To be perfectly honest, however, I admire *Little Nemo* more than I actually like it," Watterson admitted later in his essay for *The Best of Little Nemo*. "McCay was clearly more interested in his stage than in his actors, and a stage, no matter how grand, can't carry a play. The inventive visual effects notwithstanding, I can't read the strip without thinking how much more enchanting *Slumberland* would be if the characters, rather than the backdrops and costumes, advanced the story. Regrettably, the characters are cardboard dress-up dolls, devoid of spunk or wit."

Though each strip starts and ends essentially the same way, the trick is to take the audience on a different journey each time. Called an "enjoy the ride" strip by some comic historians, McCay's strip makes you realize that there's a million ways to get between point A and point B. Watterson notably utilized the same storytelling technique with his Spaceman Spiff and sled-ride sequences. Though you always knew that Calvin was going to snap out of his interstellar fantasy in the middle of an awkward situation or crash his sled, the fun of the strip is to find out what happened along the way.

Another striking similarity between the two strips is the manipulation of perception. Though Nemo is very clearly dreaming his adventures while lying in bed, he often has a psychosomatic reaction to his dream. For instance, in the dream he may be avoiding a giant mushroom, which causes him to jump off the bed in reality. Calvin had the same psychosomatic reactions — when Spaceman Spiff dodges aliens, Calvin evades his parents; when the whale breaches the ocean, Calvin shoots out of the tub.

The difference is that Calvin actively overlays his fantasy with reality. Those around him — with the exception of Hobbes — can never see what he is seeing, though they do see Calvin interacting within their realm of perception. This was one of the key revolutionary traits of *Calvin and Hobbes* and the crux of its genius. We had a chance to see what Calvin and Hobbes were seeing and what everyone else was, too. In this way, you were able to see what neither Calvin and Hobbes nor the adults could see. The strips were oftentimes two takes on the same joke with a unifying punch line. Even when you knew that it was Calvin, not a *Tyrannosaurus rex*, on a rampage you weren't sure what situation he had encountered and why a rampage was necessary until the reality was revealed at the end.

Undoubtedly, one of Calvin's most charming qualities was this ability to imagine. Like John Lennon, Calvin was a dreamer, but he wasn't the only one. The modern American dreamer archetype is arguably James Thurber's Walter Mitty from the short story, "The Secret Life of Walter Mitty." Thurber's piece for *The New Yorker* followed the absent-minded Mitty as he went through a day of running errands with his wife while he imagined himself as a hydroplane commander, a surgeon, an RAF pilot, an assassin and, finally, the victim of a firing squad. The way Mitty overlapped his imagination with reality is close to the manner in which Calvin interacts with reality. In the opening of "The Secret Life . . .," Mitty is revving up a hydroplane to get it through a storm. It soon becomes apparent that he is really just flooring his Buick to 55 mph, about 15 miles faster than his wife would prefer. Though both Calvin and Mitty are regarded as out-of-touch — or perhaps just touched — by their peers, this stops neither of them reveling in their intricate flights of fancy.

Another classic dreamer was Ralph Phillips, the star of two animated shorts for Warner Brothers' *Merrie Melodies*, "From A to Z-Z-Z-Z" and "Boyhood Daze." This pair of classic cartoons was directed by animator genius Chuck Jones, who would go on to create Saturday morning icons like Wile E. Coyote, the Road Runner and Pepe le Pew. 1954's "A to Z-Z-Z-Z" introduces our pie-eyed star, Ralph Phillips, who's daydreaming at the back of the classroom while his classmates recite the multiplication tables. He imagines himself to be a bird, then a flying boy, before his teacher interrupts his flight of fancy by waking him up. Ralph is sent to the blackboard to do a problem, but falls asleep and imagines himself a chalky hero fighting with the numbers. Then he's a cowboy-turned-postman who gets killed by Indians, a deep-sea diver who engages sharks in hand-to-hand combat, a boxer and a general who declares "I shall return," before the screen dips to black.

In 1957's "Boyhood Daze," Phillips makes good on his promise. He is banished to his room after breaking a window playing baseball. As he bemoans his bad luck, he imagines himself in alternate realities. The family cat is transformed into a tiger, much like when Hobbes the doll becomes Hobbes the tuna-loving tiger. Ralph further imagines himself as a six-shooter-toting African explorer, a jet fighter pilot and a jailbird. Ultimately, these fantasies dissolve and his father lets him go play outside again. Phillips runs down to the sunny front yard with his mitt and bat, but sees an axe next to the woodpile. In the final fantasy, he's George Washington marching over to the cherry tree with the axe.

Though there is no evidence that Watterson ever saw either cartoon or read Thurber, it's impossible to deny the similarities between these characters' imaginative lives and Calvin's. There are hints of other possible influences scattered throughout *Calvin and Hobbes*'s ten-year run — the characters' Muppet-y mouths, their *Looney Tunes*-esque acts of daredevilry and Watterson's flashes of Twain-esque humor that made you think as much as it made you laugh.

There are a couple of outright comic-strip homages in *Calvin and Hobbes*. Spaceman Spiff's adventures often recall those of *Flash Gordon* and *Buck Rogers*, while a couple of Sunday fantasies purposely mimic the style of old-school dramatic strips like *Mary Worth*, *Dr Kildare* and *Rex Morgan, MD*. The film-noir-styled adventures of Calvin's alter ego, Tracer Bullet, seemed to be a mash-up of *Detective Comics* and *Dick Tracy* (not to mention *The Maltese*

Falcon), replete with the hard-boiled dialogue. There were also a number of tips of the hat to Disney. At various times throughout the strip's run there are references to Mickey Mouse, Jiminy Cricket, Bambi and the song "Zippity Doo Da" from the 1946 Disney film *Song of the South*.

One work that sources close to Watterson assert that he didn't read until after he created *Calvin and Hobbes*, but which could easily have been an influence worth noting, was Crockett Johnson's *Barnaby*. Crockett, who also wrote the beloved children's book *Harold and His Purple Crayon*, debuted *Barnaby* in the spring of 1942, right after the United States had stepped into the fray of the Second World War. The simply drawn strip followed a little boy, Barnaby Baxter, who has a pink-winged Fairy Godfather named J. J. O'Malley. The ever-hungry godfather, who brandishes a Havana cigar as a magic wand and frequently exclaims the nonsensical phrase "Cushlamochree," can be seen only by the boy, who can't convince anyone else that he exists.

Though Crockett's spare artwork is by no means reflected in Watterson's deft figuring and lush landscaping, the central conceits of the strips are somewhat similar. Here's a boy with an imaginary friend who can affect the real world, though he was usually too lazy or ineffectual to do so. The pie-eyed boy also sometimes goes on fantastical adventures with the Fairy Godfather, though he never transforms himself into another character or alter ego.

A juxtaposition of Tigger from *Winnie the Pooh* with Hobbes yields further similarities. "Tigger is probably more naive and energetic," Watterson once admitted to *The Comics Journal*. "[B]ut he's an endearing character. Disney did a good job with him in animation, although the other *Pooh* characters suffered in the

translation. The original *Pooh* stories are very subtle and sophisticated. They went right over my head as a kid, which is why they never
were a real influence on me, but I reread them recently, and they're
hilarious. If I had understood the stories earlier, I'd have certainly
swiped the idea."

Watterson didn't limit his artistic influences with respect to time,
medium or national origin. When talking to *The Comics Journal*,
he professed to drawing inspiration from all different kinds of art.
"I enjoy the work of the German expressionists, particularly the
woodcuts of the Brücke group and Lyonel Feininger," Watterson
told the interviewer. "Egon Schiele is also a favorite. I find all of his
work very immediate and honest, and I suppose I respond most to
the directness and rawness of these images. Prints of almost any
kind have a special appeal to me. The physical difficulty in making
an image usually seems to distill it, and the artist is less able to
hide behind a lot of fancy technique. I like watercolor for the same
reason. Once it's down, you're stuck with it."

"As to what influence these and other artists have on my cartoons, I'm hard pressed to say," he continued in the same interview.
"Mainly they help me realize the many different ways one can
visually express oneself. Too often cartoonists just look at other
cartoonists and, after a lot of inbreeding, everyone has the same
funny look. The challenge of drawing is that there is no one right
way to visually describe something. It's a good thing to confront
your limitations and preconceptions every so often."

Watterson infuses *Calvin and Hobbes* with the essence of many
artistic influences without cheapening his work by indiscriminately
pilfering the corpora of other comic strips. He may have borrowed,
but he never stole, and he always transformed older ideas into

something totally his own. Plus, Watterson dreamed up tyranno-saurs flying F-14s, a cannibal snowman and a transmogrifier made out of a cardboard box — no one had ever done that before.

CHAPTER 4

A Boy and His Tiger

After watching Jack Nicklaus win the 1965 Masters, Bobby Jones said, "Nicklaus played a game with which I am not familiar." Jones meant that Nicklaus' playing was so good that he was playing a different game. And that's what Watterson was doing. *Calvin and Hobbes* was deep, funny, and true. And it hit home with so many of us who haven't left our childhoods.

— Mike Peters, creator of *Mother Goose & Grimm*

Calvin and Hobbes first appeared in approximately 35 papers around the country on 18 November 1985. In the debut strip, Calvin, wearing a pith helmet, tells his father he has rigged a tiger trap with a tuna fish sandwich. Hearing this, his dad asks him, "They like tuna fish, huh?" and Calvin responds, "Tigers will do **anything** for a tuna fish sandwich!" The last frame reveals Hobbes as a living tiger noshing away, while suspended upside down from a rope trap in a tree commenting, "We're kind of stupid that way." At this point, Hobbes is depicted only as an actual tiger and the fantasy conceit remains unknown to the reader, who takes Hobbes, the living tiger, at face value.

In the next day's strip, Calvin asks his father what he should do when he catches a tiger and his father exasperatedly tells him to bring it home and stuff it. Calvin misinterprets this advice, which produces the gag of the strip: Calvin overfeeding Hobbes in the kitchen. There is still no intimation that Hobbes is anything other than a real, living, breathing and voraciously eating tiger. It's not until the third strip that Calvin's private reality is revealed. His father comes upstairs to complain about the noise he was hearing after Calvin is supposed to be asleep. Calvin blames it on Hobbes, who he claims is jumping on the bed. The father responds, ""Hobbes" was **not** jumping on the bed! Now go to sleep!" Not only do we learn the tiger's name, but there is also the important epiphany for the reader: Calvin sees his friend as a living tiger, while his father only sees him as a doll.

The Universal sales team was initially worried about how to sell this dual reality, so they drew up promotional packets to crystallize the premise simply for the uninitiated. "To Calvin, Hobbes is everything a child could ask for in a friend: playmate, co-conspirator, sounding board," the pitch explains. "To everyone else, Hobbes is a stuffed tiger."

Once readers are in on the joke, they are quickly thrown into Calvin's unique world. The first color Sunday strip found the less-than-intrepid duo worrying that there were monsters under the bed. After being placated by Calvin's father and arming themselves, they are suddenly confronted by what they think is a monster in the hallway. After honking a horn and shooting it with a dart gun to frighten it away, the monster is revealed to be Calvin's understandably angry father. Calvin's mother is introduced to readers two days later when she refuses to allow the six-year-old Calvin drive the family car. This is the family. One mom, one dad and one kid who doesn't want to let go of his stuffed animal.

Calvin's first use of an alter ego occurs less than two weeks into the existence of the strip on 29 November 1985. This watershed moment is also the reader's introduction to Calvin's school; his teacher, Ms Wormwood; and his principal, Principal Spittle (though neither one is named at that time in the strip). In it, Calvin is sent to the principal's office for not paying attention. As he walks there, he envisions himself as Spaceman Spiff who has been captured by aliens who want to torture him for the "secret formula to the atomic napalm neutralizer." In the thrall of this imagining Calvin panics and as the two astonished school officials look on in the final frame, the principal asks, "Why is he eating his hall pass?"

Another major supporting character is introduced within the first month: Calvin's neighbor and potential love interest, Susie Derkins. First alluded to on 3 December 1985, mentioned by name on 4 December and finally seen on 5 December, Susie is the new girl in the neighborhood. Their initial interactions are of the classic "I'm pulling your hair because I like you" variety, since Calvin insults her and tries to gross her out even as he exhibits a subtle interest. Over time, however, their relationship develops beyond any semblance of desire and they remain fully combative with one another for the remainder of the strip's run, though Hobbes always enjoys Susie's attentions.

However, Watterson wasn't worried about future storylines or character development when the strip premiered. "My concern was really very basic: whether the strip would make enough in sales so it could continue," Watterson told *Editor & Publisher* in 1986. These characters he had created lived in a fragile world. Though there was the potential for cartoonists to earn a six-figure salary if they were syndicated in enough papers, sold books and allowed merchandise to be licensed, this was not the norm for working cartoonists. Many earned far less than that and had to find other freelance work just to subsist. More importantly, if enough newspapers didn't pick up your strip, the syndicate might eventually drop you, which would put you back outside the game entirely. And trying to get back in was even harder than trying to get in the first time.

Despite these daunting odds and dim prospects — and a firm warning from his editor at Universal, Lee Salem — Watterson immediately quit his day job doing layout in January 1986. "There was too much at stake," West revealed to me. "He wanted to give everything he had to *Calvin and Hobbes*. If it didn't work out, it didn't work out, but it wasn't going to be because he had to spend eight hours a day laying out the damn *Pennysaver*." Sadly, being syndicated in a small number of newspapers pulled in the same paltry amount of money he had earned as a layout artist.

A couple of months after that, he also stopped drawing editorial cartoons for the *Sun* — a job he had been doing for six years by then. Fellow cartoonist Jeff Darcy remembers getting a call from their editor-in-chief. "I picked up and the voice said, "Hey, Watterson's not going to be doing our cartoons anymore. Would you like to be our editorial cartoonist full time?" So I've always said his good fortune was my good fortune." Darcy wasn't surprised by the decision: "It always struck me that his sole goal was to be a comic-strip artist, not an editorial cartoonist."

When Darcy took the position, he sent Watterson a note to see if he had any tips for him and to pick his brain, but never got any response. "Which I thought was very standoffish," he told me. "Another hint I got of that standoffishness came from some of the reporters there. One of them told me, "It's cool how you talk to us and how you're willing to talk. I worked in the office where Watterson used to bring his cartoons in and he didn't want to talk to anybody." It's interesting that this attitude predates his *Calvin and Hobbes* fame — even back then he was just a surly cartoonist." Despite this characterization, Darcy defends Watterson's choice to avoid attention by personalizing his perceived standoffishness. "When you have someone who's aloof and reclusive, people tend to say, "Well, he's a jerk." But I can be reclusive and aloof, and I don't think it's because I'm a jerk. It's in my nature."

Quitting the steady paychecks and relying on *Calvin and Hobbes*'s success was definitely a gamble. Not a reckless, "put it all on 34 and spin the wheel" gamble, but more of a calculated bet rooted in principle, rather than greed. Watterson considered himself an artist, not an employee who happened to draw cartoons for a living, and he wanted to make sure *Calvin and Hobbes* fulfilled his considerable vision. At the Kenyon commencement speech he gave in 1990, Watterson spoke about how his difficult journey to syndication gave him a gravitas about his art. "Drawing comic strips for five years without pay drove home the point that the fun of cartooning wasn't in the money; it was in the work," Watterson declared. Lucky for him, it quickly felt as if the work was paying off.

Though the syndicate had cautioned Watterson not to get too excited, initial feedback indicated that the strip was going to be a hit. The first sign of success was when a number of papers signed up for it within the first three months of publication, making it Universal's second largest launch after *For Better or For Worse* in 1979, and that comic strip had become a bona fide smash. "We knew it was something different and something remarkable," Salem says now. "But I don't think anyone projected 2,500 newspapers at that point. We did know we had a very, very good feature with a lot of sales potential on our hands, though, because we were getting calls from newspaper editors saying, "We heard you've got this strip," even though the sales people may have not made it out to that territory yet. That's unheard of in this business."

"The buzz was immediate," comic-strip writer and comic historian Brian Walker recalls now. Cartooning is in Walker's blood — his father is *Beetle Bailey* and *Hi and Lois* creator Mort Walker. "Everybody was saying, "Have you seen this strip? This is great,"" he told me. "A lot of my father's friends from his generation don't seem to like anything new that comes out, but they were impressed." There were already a lot of long-running, successful strips in the paper like *Peanuts*, *Garfield* and *Blondie*, "But everybody moved over and made room for him, because the talent was obvious," Walker remembered.

It took almost six months, but the strip finally appeared in Watterson's local paper, the *Plain Dealer*, on Sunday, 2 March 1986. Until that point, his friends never had any real proof of his employment. "They probably think I'm selling drugs," he quipped to the *Plain Dealer*, in an article entitled "Cartoon caprices: artist finally draws a winner," which ran the day before the strip appeared and featured a rare picture of the cartoonist at his drawing board. Watterson also contributed a cartoon of himself sitting at the same drawing board, chiding his creations: "C'mon kid, do something funny. I've got a deadline." Calvin responds with his usual churlish bravado: "Maybe I don't feel inspired. What's it worth to you?"

Though Watterson clearly comes across in this article as thrilled with *Calvin and Hobbes*'s early success, he also expressed some wariness over his unexpected fame. He reveals that he almost instantly started getting fan mail when the strip started, along with requests for autographs and original art. "They all want something," he declared. "It was kind of disturbing at first. It surprises me . . . that there's any element of fame in this." West concurs, "The success of *Calvin and Hobbes* caught him by surprise. He wasn't standing there waiting for the parade to begin; his expectations were very modest. All he wanted to do was be able to earn a living doing what he loved."

Unlike cartoonists such as *Garfield* creator Jim Davis or *Peanuts* creator Charles Schulz, both of whom embraced public life, Watterson didn't gravitate towards center stage. Lee Salem remembers that the young cartoonist very quickly decided to limit his public exposure and begrudgingly agreed to do only a handful of interviews and appearances to promote the strip. By everyone's accounts, Watterson wanted to concentrate solely on *Calvin and Hobbes*; anything else was a distraction that degraded the quality of the strip and his ability to produce it sanely.

His dedication and hard work paid off. Within a year of the strip's launching, *Calvin and Hobbes* was in 160 papers, and in another six months that number had doubled to over 300 papers. The cartooning community was taking notice of this new wunderkind, too. One of Watterson's cartoons was featured at the prestigious 1986 Festival of Cartoon Art at Ohio State University, alongside works by cartooning greats like Milton Caniff, Hank Ketchum and his old friend Jim Borgman.

All these accolades meant more and more attention from the public, which disturbed the reserved young artist. Watterson talked about this transition period in his introduction to *The Complete Calvin and Hobbes*: "As happy as I was that the strip seemed to be catching on, I was not prepared for the resulting attention. Cartoonists are a very low grade of celebrity, but any amount of it is weird. Besides disliking the diminishment of privacy and the inhibiting quality of feeling watched, I valued my anonymous, boring life. In fact, I didn't see how I could write honestly without it."

It was to cut down on these intrusions that Watterson and his wife made the move to nearby Hudson, Ohio, in 1986. They rented a small four-room house, where Bill took over a spare room as his studio. In this private place, he would slave over the strips before mailing them into the syndicate. The new surroundings allowed Watterson to concentrate on *Calvin and Hobbes* almost exclusively, while still remaining close to his family and childhood friends.

It was exceedingly difficult work, especially in the age before Photoshop and email. In those days, if you messed up, you couldn't just undo a series of mistakes with a couple of deft clicks of your mouse or send your strips in at the last minute. To begin his artistic process, Watterson would sit down and "stare into space for an hour and sometimes not come up with a single decent idea, or sometimes no idea at all," as he wrote in *Sunday Pages 1985–1995*. "[I]t's very tempting to go do something else or just draw up a strip, but I find that if I make myself stick to it for another hour I can sometimes come up with several good ideas." He would write these ideas down in a notebook. After self-editing and rewriting the concepts until he felt happy with the results, he would then doodle a rough idea for the visual elements of the strip. "I really enjoy taking a big chunk of time and working on the drawing and nothing else," Watterson continued in the *Sunday Pages*. "That allows me to make sure that I'm really challenging the art, making each picture as interesting as I can . . . stick in a close-up or an odd perspective."

All this careful preparation was by no means a guarantee that an idea would become an actual strip, because Watterson set a high quality bar. "Sometimes I just cross the whole thing out," he wrote in *The Calvin and Hobbes Tenth Anniversary Book*. "On occasion, I've ripped up entire stories — weeks of material — that I didn't think were good." Watterson told Lee Nordling for his book *Your Career in Comics*, "The quality of a strip is . . . determined by the quantity of ideas in the wastebasket. Every cartoonist writes a lot of bad strips, and the never-ending pressure to meet deadlines encourages cartoonists to publish virtually everything they think up. The only way to resist that pressure is to stay far enough ahead of the deadlines that you can throw away mediocre material and write something better."

"He always underestimated his talent and he's not entirely convinced of it," West told me when I asked him about Watterson's artistic process. "Bill was never quite sure if he was as good as other people told him he was. He worked very hard to prove it, both to himself and others. That's one of the keys to why *Calvin and Hobbes* was so great. It's because he never gave up. When other cartoonists would have been satisfied with that first idea of the day, he discarded it, and then discarded the next one, and discarded the next one. He waited till he got it right." Sometimes getting it right meant trashing weeks' and weeks' worth of ideas that other cartoonists might have felt compelled to run in order to meet deadlines, but Watterson tried to avoid that situation by staying as far ahead of the curve as possible. "[I]f you're right up against the deadline, there's no quality control," Watterson griped to Lee Nordling. "It's just garbage in, garbage out. I've been in that situation, and it's miserable."

After he weeded out all the weakest ideas, he would show the self-approved, roughed-out strips to his wife, who would suggest changes or reject further strips. After this final edit, Watterson would ink up the ideas that he liked the most out of the remaining contenders. First he sketched in the dialogue using a 2H pencil, then he penciled in the rough outlines of the characters. Finally, he would draw the strip using India ink with a sable brush on Strathmore Bristol board, using a Rapidograph fountain pen to ink in the dialogue. He could only do about six daily strips or a single Sunday strip in a day's work.

If the strip was a color Sunday, there was yet another step. Watterson would put a transparent plastic overlay on the black-and-white ink drawing, then paint it. But since a newspaper's color palette was limited, he would choose from the 64 colors offered for the comics (it would increase to 125 by the early '90s) and indicate which he would like used; these originals were turned into color negatives. Finally, the strips were mailed to the syndicate, where Lee would check the spelling and keep an eye out for potentially offensive material. David Bowe remembered one strip in which Calvin was a grenade-throwing terrorist that didn't make the cut with the syndicate, though they allowed strips to run that featured a snowman committing suicide (he put a hot-water bottle on his head) and Calvin throwing up a Nazi salute.

After all these edits and rewrites the strips would finally run, oftentimes months after Watterson had the original idea for them. It was a time-consuming process and one that Watterson rarely allowed to be interrupted. He made an exception in the fall of 1986, to take a trip over to Ohio State University's Festival of Cartooning. It was there that writer Richard Ellers of the *Plain Dealer* caught up with him and his wife. Ellers was hesitant to approach the couple at first, but managed to convince the usually reticent cartoonist to do a casual interview over lunch at a local diner while his wife looked on. The trio had a relaxed meal and Ellers recalls Watterson's wife as "very nice and very funny," who at one point referred to Watterson as "my Calvin."

After the meal was eaten, it came time to take a picture for the article and Watterson balked. Since his picture had appeared in the *Plain Dealer* in March, he had been besieged by well-wishers and autograph seekers whenever he went out. He had no desire to be a celebrity and had decided not to have any further pictures circulated in the public domain. Thinking quickly, Ellers suggested a novel workaround.

Grabbing a pen and paper, he had Watterson quickly sketch a picture of Calvin. The artist then held it up in front of his face, leaving only his bespectacled eyes and the crew-cut top of his head exposed. The results are the clever masking of a man by his creation; a metaphor that the publicity-shy Watterson couldn't have missed. After the shot was snapped, he signed the drawing and gave it to Ellers. Today, that sketch is lost in his attic and he sounded shocked to learn that it was worth thousands of dollars.

The resulting article, "Calvin has cartoonist by the tail," ran in the *Cleveland Plain Dealer* on 5 October 1986. In what might be his most relaxed and candid interview, Watterson talks about his desire for anonymity candidly: "We're very private people," he told Ellers between bites. "I like our isolated experience." He also claimed that he answered every piece of fan mail he received. "I need the letters to keep in touch," he asserted. "The mail lets me know what works and what doesn't."

Watterson also touched on where he might take his comic strip in the future. "As outrageous as Calvin is, I have to keep his character consistent," he told Ellers. "Calvin may be outrageous, but I couldn't go to an extreme, say, and make him a mass murderer . . . I get an idea for a situation, then I sit back and see how Calvin and Hobbes work it out. I never know what's going to happen; sometimes it's even a surprise to me."

Though he retired years ago, Ellers retains very fond memories of his interviewee. "He was such an interesting character," he told me by phone from his home in Warren, Ohio. "In retrospect, he was probably the one guy I'd have liked to have hung out with after work the most. Just man to man; not reporter to writer. Just two guys fishing or something."

The next interaction Watterson had with the press didn't go nearly as well. The *Los Angeles Times* assigned writer Paul Dean to do a piece on Watterson in the spring of 1987 that they hoped would be a definitive profile. In a way it was, but not in the way they had imagined. The resulting article, "Calvin and Hobbes creator draws on the simple life," found Watterson with his hackles raised. "*Calvin and Hobbes* will not exist intact if I do not exist intact," Watterson told Dean. "And I will not exist intact if I have to put up with all this stuff."

"I enjoy the isolation [from people], that's how I work," he continued. "I read an article on Garrison Keillor where he said that fame has, to a certain extent, corrupted his work. He gets some of his inspiration from being an unrecognized observer. But if he can't walk into a hardware store and overhear people and be inconspicuous, he can't get his material."

After the interview, Watterson called Lee Salem and told him he didn't want to do any more press. None. Nothing. Nada. "There was a tone in the questions that he found insulting," Salem says now. "And the reality is if you had an open door policy with any reporter who came along, you'd soon get a call from your syndicate saying, "Where the hell is the work?"" Salem added with a chuckle. "It's the panel of the strip that should interest people, not what kind of coffee the cartoonist has in the morning."

Despite Watterson's reticence to embrace his own success, he continued to gain the raves of his readers and his peers. Around this time, he was a surprise winner at the National Cartoonist Society's Reuben Awards for "Outstanding Cartoonist of the Year." What made this even more unforeseeable was that Watterson wasn't even a NCS member, and its awards usually went to established dues-payers.

Uncomfortable with the recognition he was receiving, Watterson didn't attend the ceremony at New York City's Plaza Hotel on 23 May 1987; Universal Press Syndicate president John P. McMeel accepted the trophy on his behalf. According to *Editor & Publisher*, who called Watterson at home in Ohio at the time, he said, "I'm very flattered. To be held in esteem by my peers is very gratifying," and admitted that he had been "caught off guard" by the award.

That year saw the release of Watterson's first book, entitled simply *Calvin and Hobbes*. All the strips are reproduced in black and white, including the Sundays, though Watterson did an exclusive watercolor that wraps around the cover of the book. The amusing artwork captures the pair suspended in mid-air. Hobbes, the driver of the wagon they just rode off the end of the dock, is looking apprehensively down at the water. Calvin, attached by a rope to the wagon, is wearing roller skates and clutching an umbrella, gleefully smiling, perhaps believing in that instant he is actually flying.

The collection is dedicated to Watterson's wife, Melissa, and the dedication page features a celebratory Hobbes with a big grin, lifting his party hat in salute while he charmingly offers a flower. Garry Trudeau wrote the introduction and used the space to wax poetic about Watterson's rare abilities, dubbing him the "reporter who's gotten it right." This was high praise coming from a cartoonist who sometimes tells more truth than any other writer in the papers he's published in. "Anyone who's done time with a small child knows that reality can be highly situational," Trudeau continued. "The utterance which an adult knows to be a "lie" may well reflect a child's deepest conviction, at least at the moment it pops out. Fantasy is so accessible, and it is joined with such force and frequency, that resentful parents like Calvin's assume they are being manipulated, when the truth is far more frightening: they don't even exist. The child is both king and keeper of this realm, and he can be very choosy about the company he keeps."

Watterson's book publisher, Andrews and McMeel, proposed that the artist go on a brief three-week tour to promote the collection. His somewhat acerbic reply was that he would be game for a zero-week-long tour and he refused to do any publicity. In spite of Watterson's refusal to promote the book, the first printing of 50,000 quickly sold out and *Calvin and Hobbes* went on to sell over a million copies. After that, every one of his books had an initial printing of at least a million copies.

A year later, Watterson solidified his success when he published *Something Under the Bed Is Drooling* in 1988. This collection stayed on the best-seller list for almost a year. Watterson's old acquaintance, Pulitzer Prize-winning editorial cartoonist Pat Oliphant, who was also syndicated through Universal, wrote the foreword.

After declaring that there "is a mystical quality to Bill Watterson's work," Oliphant compares Watterson's abilities to those of George Herriman and Walt Kelly. He ends the introduction with a rhetorical question. "You want magic? Watterson the alchemist has conjured forth a work of subtlety, character, and depth far out of proportion to his tender years. I wish him long life, and may the powers of his sorcery never diminish. You want magic? This is a collection of the sorcerer's recipes for changing simple ink and paper into the purest gold . . . This book is pure magic." As a thank you for the kind words, Watterson sent Oliphant an original strip that he simply signed, "Best wishes, Watterson." "He didn't wear his heart on his sleeve," Oliphant says with a laugh.

A year after the phenomenal success of *Something Under the Bed Is Drooling*, Watterson won a Reuben Award for the second time, making him the youngest two-time winner in the Society's history. Once again Watterson did not appear at the ceremony, leaving Universal Press Syndicate's vice-president Kathleen Andrews and Lee Salem to accept the award on his behalf. Watterson's only comment on the accolade was a press release sound bite that was probably written by his publicist, "I am very flattered and honored to have my work recognized by my colleagues."

I spoke with close to 50 cartoonists for this project and a number were either perplexed or offended to varying degrees by the fact that Watterson didn't personally accept either award. "We all wanted to congratulate him," *For Better or Worse* creator Lynn Johnston said simply, when I talked with her from her studio in Canada. "We were hurt by his no-show. That's one night out of your life, so who cares? On Monday morning, who cares? We're all back to work. Though some people might say they were offended, I think it was more disappointment, because they all wanted to look at him, touch him and congratulate him." Brian Walker added in a separate interview, "All the cartoonists respected his talent, but a lot of us were puzzled by his paranoia about coming out in the public."

By this time, almost 900 papers were carrying the strip and it was being published around the world in a number of languages. However, the names Calvin and Hobbes did not always translate well, so the duo was known as Steen and Stoffer in Denmark (where Stupendous Man was known as Sluppermand), Lassi and Leevi in Finland, Kazmer and Huba in Hungary, Kalfin and Gopsya in Belarus, Max and Mauli in Switzerland, Tommy and Tigern in Norway (where Susie was renamed Marianne), and Kelvin and Celsjusz in Poland.

Despite his huge success, there is little in the public record about Watterson from this period. The more popular his work became, the less of himself he offered to his audience. This is as frustrating as it is fascinating. It also made me cast my net wider, as I began to examine Watterson's contemporaries in greater detail.

The late '80s were an exciting time for the comics page. Not only was *Calvin and Hobbes* a phenomenon, but there was a wealth of other material for readers to wake up to every morning. Gary Larson's offbeat one-panel *The Far Side* was on a side-splitting hot streak, while Berke Breathed's *Bloom County* (and, later, *Outland*) was a surreal, sarcastic acid trip of a comic strip that had turned into an unexpected hit.

There were more women drawing than ever before, and finding larger audiences. Lynn Johnston's acclaimed family strip *For Better or Worse* tackled death, coming out and teenage angst in a richly real and emotional way, while Cathy Guisewite's *Cathy* perfectly skewered the life of a young, single woman. Garry Trudeau's *Doonesbury* was on a winning run lampooning George H. W. Bush and Oliver North as the Iran-Contra affair unfolded. Even established cartoonists were reaching new heights. *Peanuts* underwent a critical renaissance and *Garfield* became even more popular as its creator, Jim Davis, found new ways to merchandise his orange and black striped character.

Despite the competition, however, it was *Calvin and Hobbes*, *The Far Side* and *Bloom County/Outland* which truly seized the public's imagination and made the comics relevant again. This unconventional trifecta was the Holy Trinity of comic strips in the late '80s and until the mid-'90s. No one else came close. And though none of these three cartoonists could have known it, they were at the forefront of the last Golden Age of American newspaper comics.

This trio never made any joint public appearances, but they certainly knew of and respected each other. Watterson corresponded with Berke Breathed frequently, and when he did give interviews often mentioned him with great affection. Though there's no evidence that Watterson ever corresponded with Larson, he did include a homage to him in a special watercolor he created to accompany a 1987 interview with the *Plain Dealer Magazine*. Calvin and Hobbes are sitting under a tree reading the issue in which Watterson's interview appears. The headline proclaims "Comics shrunk again!" and lie next to the funny pages, while Calvin gripes, "The Sunday magazine is really slipping. Look at the geek they interviewed **this** time." Hobbes replies, "See if you can find where they buried "The Far Side."" Though this was not an official *Calvin and Hobbes* strip, it does mark the only time that Watterson invoked another cartoon by name in his published work.

Around that same time, Watterson discussed Larson's genius with *Honk!* Magazine: "I really like the lunacy of *The Far Side*," he's quoted as saying. "I do enjoy [Larson's] stuff a lot." And in an interview with *The Comics Journal*, he threw out another compliment: "*The Far Side* is [a] great [strip]. I laugh out loud at this strip more than any other. The drawings somehow suit it exactly. Wonderful stuff."

Like Watterson, I thought *The Far Side* was wonderful stuff. My mother still has on her fridge the strip with the couple splayed out on their living-room floor. Its caption, "The Arnolds feign death until the Wagners, sensing awkwardness, are compelled to leave," makes me chortle every time. Larson had an ability to write quirky one-liners that felt more like *New Yorker* cartoons drawn on a tab of LSD than simple gag-a-days. Though he was not the most stunning of artists, his off-kilter characters and surrealist takes on the world fit his unorthodox sense of humor perfectly. You were never quite sure what you were going to get when you checked out the latest installment, but you knew it would never be mundane or expected, which is an accomplishment when it's juxtaposed with repetitive fare such as *The Family Circus* and *Andy Capp*.

I tried to find any reference Gary Larson might have made to Bill Watterson or *Calvin and Hobbes*, but did not find a single word. I thought this would be easy — like trying to find a quote from Mick Jagger about John Lennon — but it was as impossible as trying to find Abe Lincoln commenting on his favorite contestants from the second season of *Flavor of Love*. It turns out that Larson never gave many interviews when he was cartooning and gave even fewer once he had retired.

So, after combing the internet and rereading the few interviews with Gary Larson I could locate, I resolved to try to get in touch with him for an interview. He hadn't given one in over two years, but I was curious enough to give it a go. I was already trying to find the Salinger of cartooning, so why not try to get its Stanley Kubrick on the phone, too?

Since Larson's retirement, his strips have been licensed on everything from calendars to coffee mugs, so it was easy enough finding contact information for FarWorks, Inc., the company that oversees the licensing of Larson's work. It's equally easy to find the press-shy cartoonist's address through a public records search. However, any attempt to get the man on the phone — or on a computer — turned out to be futile. An assistant from his firm wrote back to decline my request and the letter I sent to his home was neither returned nor answered.

Although I knew talking to Larson would be hard, this turn of events left me somewhat depressed. However, my spirits were buoyed when I got an email from Berke Breathed shortly thereafter, agreeing to an interview. It was a watershed moment, because he became the first major cartoonist from Watterson's era to speak to me. I had an inspiring hour-long interview, filled with great anecdotes and analysis. His comments on Watterson were as self-deprecatingly amusing as they were insightful. "Watterson reminded me daily that my own success was built on a flimsy foundation of fraud and cultural timeliness," Breathed confessed. "I walked in as the half-talent that I was and found that the comic page was waiting for the only thing that I overwhelmingly shone at: a smart-ass attitude. Certainly not good comic art."

Watterson was a fan of Breathed, even before he had made his acquaintance. In issue 12 of Rich West's *Target* magazine, Watterson had reviewed Breathed's collection 'Toons for the Times, along with editorial cartoonist Jules Feiffer's collection *Marriage is an Invasion of Privacy and Other Dangerous Views*. Watterson's compliments to the artists are interwoven as he draws parallels between their divergent works. "Rather than conform to customary conceits of what editorial cartoons and comic strips should be, these artists thrash out into new territory," Watterson opined. "The zip in their work comes from this integrity, their unwillingness to compromise, even when to do so might make their work more immediately palatable for the masses. They challenge themselves, and they challenge their readers. It's more work on both sides of the cartoon, but artist and audience alike come out the richer for it."

Several years after this review, Watterson brought up Breathed again in an interview with *The Comics Journal*. "I enjoy *Bloom County*'s unpredictability and irreverence," he declared. "In a generally brain-dead comics page, I usually find *Bloom County*'s to-hell-with-everybody anarchy refreshing. Opus, of course, is an inspired character."

"I luxuriated in Bill's graphic flights of fancy," Breathed told me. "The planets, the monsters, the imagination of a little boy. For me, his work was of most interest when he was drawing something wonderful or ridiculous." Breathed and Watterson became acquaintances by mail in the late '80s and early '90s, when they started corresponding about taking ownership of their strips back from their syndicates. However, it was not a friendship that ever extended beyond the page. "Except for some marvelously twisted and sick drawings that he would add to the bottom of his letters — mostly at my or my characters' expense — I can't say I ever got to know him," Breathed admitted. "From most reports and reported anecdotes . . .

he is most assuredly a serious whack job. I say that with enormous affection. I work toward this myself every day."

One of Watterson's casual sketches made it into the final *Outland* collection, *One Last Little Peek*. The cartoon shows a raging, sunglasses-wearing Breathed in a motorboat, stuffing money into the gas tank. He's booting Mickey Mouse and Ronald-Ann Smith from *Bloom County* off the front of the boat, while screaming, "Lazy freeloaders! I said none of you ride until your faces are on boxer shorts! Who do you think you are? The @*#@!! Simpsons?! Get to work!" On the dock above him, a corpulent syndicate executive in an ill-fitting suit is gleefully rubbing his hands together and thinking to himself, "Heh heh . . . I'll have this boy back in the palm of my hand in **no** time."

"That strip was good because it was emblematic of Watterson in every way," Breathed told me. "He had a vicious sense of humor that you rarely got to see in the strip. And he was highly opinionated, which you also didn't see in the strip." This would not be the only time that Watterson made an appearance in one of Breathed's compilations. In 2004, Breathed published *OPUS: 25 Years of His Sunday Best* and included a self-skewering reference to Watterson's work. The introduction to the collection showcased a 1981 *Bloom County* Sunday strip in which Milo Bloom is piloting a spaceship with a beautiful woman behind him, while he's getting shot at by the evil kitchen empire. However, he suddenly wakes up and he's at the front of his class, his hand inappropriately wrapped around his teacher's legs.

"You'll note that it features a little blonde-haired boy with an over-tweaked imagination working out his real-life anxieties and passions via space hero fantasies," Breathed wrote in the accompanying essay.

"Now *that's* a ripping Good Idea to build a comic strip around!" "So naturally I only drew this one panel," he continued. "Most new comic strips don't survive such an epic blunder. And *Bloom County* would've headed for oblivion had I not, the following week, drawn a mumbling penguin sitting on an ottoman watching TV." Thank the gods for that happy mistake!

It was these three strips that made the comics section something to anticipate happily. So even when the front page was nothing but bad news and the weather forecast called for rain, there was always something to make you smile. Watterson especially knew how to deliver a thoughtful mixture of Zen koans and punch lines. His strips were mini-meditations that gave you a moment of pause before the day shot into fast forward. They were a great way to start afresh every day.

CHAPTER 5

Calvin in Wonderland

I was simply humbled by Watterson. The way he draws dinosaurs and trees should humble anyone. I have aspired to capture things the way he does, because he has such a strong sense of action, fun and imagination.
— Nicholas Gurewitch, creator of *The Perry Bible Fellowship*

Where do you begin when you're peering through the looking glass at Calvin's wonderland? It's hard to take in and sort through ten years of *Calvin and Hobbes.* That's 3,160 strips full of jokes, abominable snowmen, daydreams, epiphanies, calls to the hardware store with unusual requests, and so much more. I am bound to leave something out — probably more than one something — leaving you, my reader, disgusted or perhaps even shaking your fist at these pages. This task is made all the more difficult by the fact that Watterson kept working at expanding the possibilities of the strip and enriching the world we came to love. His talent as a writer and artist allows the strip's audience to become lost in the lush cartoon universe he created.

Looking back, almost a decade and half since the duo's last sled ride, identifying the Calvin that lingers behind is important.

Perpetually six, Calvin is your average boy magnified by a hundred. With an imagination that works overtime and a deep-seated desire to cause as much trouble as humanly possible, Calvin did what normal boys do, but he does it with a flair and intensity that elevates the innate excitement and joy of childhood.

He loves getting up early on Saturday so he can wolf down bowls of Chocolate Frosted Sugar Bombs and watch cartoons (he enjoys the "idiots, explosives, and falling anvils"). He has an unquenchable thirst for comic books and gory B-movies of questionable moral fiber — *Cannibal Stewardess Vixens Unchained*, *Venusian Vampire Vixens*, *Attack of the Coed Cannibals*, *Vampire Sorority Babes*, *Killer Prom Queen* and *Sorority Row Horror* — watching them whenever he can get away with it (an ambition that doesn't sound so different from my own teenage love of hard R-rated sci-fi flicks like *2069: A Sex Odyssey*, *She Wolves of the Wasteland* and *Cinderella 2000*). And Calvin listens to all the vinyl he can get his hands on, from classical music and easy listening tunes to the not-so-dulcet sounds of Scrambled Debutante, whose songs glorify "depraved violence, mindless sex, and the deliberate abuse of dangerous drugs" and appeal to the inner libertine in all of us.

During the first five years of *Calvin and Hobbes*, Calvin demonstrated a working knowledge of the era he ostensibly never grew old in, the mid- to late '80s. He referenced Bugs Bunny, Don Johnson and ZZ Top as well as Dr Doom, Scrabble and Miller beer. Not to be outclassed, there were also the more highbrow references to the 1812 Overture, Paul Gauguin and Kafka. Over time, Watterson leeched out any overt cultural references, perhaps fearing that they would ultimately date the strip. "I think he would say that some of those earlier references smacked of the gag-like culture that he is inherently repelled by in American comic strips," West acknowledged. "A gag without an underpinning, without subtext, without some humanity in it, does not hold any interest to him."

The later strips without the dated allusions possess a timeless quality both in the writing and the art. During the last few years of the strip's run, you can't even tell when and where Calvin is living; the strip has been transported to a place outside of time and impervious to its degenerative effects. The family resides in a nameless, cookie-cutter suburb in the Midwest (probably Ohio, though Watterson would never confirm it); their house, car and clothes are generic. Calvin's parents are gleeful Luddites who pride themselves on their lack of conveniences. Although they have a television and a telephone, their models wouldn't have been out of place in the 1950s. Watterson admitted in interviews that he himself had a small black-and-white television in the '80s not unlike the one with bunny ears and manual dials seen in the strip.

Watterson kept all of his set pieces and flourishes simple. A perfect example of this minimalist approach is Calvin's favorite toy — a large, empty cardboard box. With a marker and some imagination, that brown square becomes a time machine, a transmogrifier, a duplicator and an Atomic Cerebral Enhance-O-Tron, to name just a few. In it, Calvin flies into the prehistoric past, is transformed into a tiger, makes several clones of himself and inflates his head with a supercharged brain. And all it requires is a large, empty cardboard box.

Taking his wagon or sled down ill-advised slopes that would make Evel Knievel wince was another one of Calvin's simple, archetypal pastimes. "Calvin's wagon is a simple device to add some physical comedy in the strip," Watterson revealed in *The Calvin and*

Hobbes Tenth Anniversary Book. "I most often use it when Calvin gets longwinded or philosophical. I think the action lends a silly counterpoint to the text, and it's a lot more interesting to draw than talking heads." Whether the duo were going off the edge of a ravine or weaving down snow-drenched hills, these playful excursions served as a simple reminder that all you need to have fun is someone just as crazy as you are.

In this way, Calvin and Hobbes often create their own diversions. Of these diversions, Calvinball is probably their favorite. The rules of the game are simple: one, there are no rules; and two, you can never play the game the same way twice. Instead, players have to quickly come up with rules that give them the best advantage over their adversaries. The on-the-fly rules are often as nonsensical as they are original. An invisible zone, a vortex spot, a bonus box, a boomerang zone and a perimeter of wisdom are just a few of the methods they devised. Combining elements of croquet, capture the flag, dodgeball and the Electric Kool Aid Acid Tests, Calvinball is as confounding as it is fantastical. Even the scoring doesn't make sense; in one game, the score is Q to 12.

Of course, no young boy's life would be complete without a secret club and Calvin and Hobbes have GROSS (Get Rid Of Slimy girlS). According to Watterson, GROSS was based on clubs he formed with his neighbor growing up. In *The Calvin and Hobbes Tenth Anniversary Book*, he describes a plan they concocted to throw hickory nuts at a neighborhood girl (a scheme Calvin and Hobbes also attempt). So they stashed a suitcase full of nuts in a tree and promptly forgot about it for six months. When they finally remembered their intentions and went back to get the suitcase, it was destroyed and the nuts were a rotting mess. "Our great plans often had this kind of boring anticlimax," Watterson joked. "Which is why fiction comes in so handy."

Most of the time, GROSS is a front for the pair to hang out in their tree house and conceive elaborate, usually doomed, plots against Susie. These brainstorming sessions often devolve into infighting, however, and their schemes are rarely realized. They go to great lengths to make tri-cornered paper hats, write flowery, self-aggrandizing poetry, draw up detailed maps and create intricate codes. After all, is there a better way to fritter away long summer days?

Throughout all of this, Calvin and Hobbes are as inseparable as they are distinct, like the id and super-ego, yin and yang and Abbott and Costello. One without the other is like peanut butter without jelly, C-3PO without R2-D2 or Jagger without Richards. "Each is funnier in contrast to the other than they would be by themselves," Watterson admitted to *The Comics Journal*. More importantly, they relied on each other for their very survival. If Hobbes wasn't there, Calvin would have no one with whom he could share his subjective reality. Likewise, if Calvin wasn't there, then everyone would see Hobbes as a mere doll, lifeless and lacking autonomy or self-determination.

Watterson uses the changeability of Calvin to tell stories from a multitude of perspectives without having to expand his cast. The blonde-haired six-year-old becomes everything from a T-rex and a robot to an eagle, a lightning bolt, a living X-ray, a shark, a tornado and a planet (though Hobbes never changes). The drawing style also differs, depending on the subject matter. It can range from a noir film and a film negative to a childish sketch or a Neo-Cubist painting (inspired by Watterson's "tendency to examine issues until

I'm incapacitated by the persuasiveness of all sides," as he wrote in *Sunday Pages 1985–1995*). Watterson playfully and artistically placed his protagonists in situations that would have been impossible in a traditional suburban family strip.

At other times, Watterson would play with Calvin's size, making him microscopic at one point and larger than our solar system at another. "You take your size for granted," he wrote by way of explanation in *Sunday Pages 1985–1995*. "You get larger up to a point and then you stop, and then that is your size, and you relate to the world from that viewpoint. If size was a complete variable, what would the world be like? In other words, if there was not a hard and fast rule of growth, how would things change? That presents me with an awful lot of visual possibilities that I enjoy working with. And to adults who are used to thinking of the world from a certain vantage point, it sometimes seems fresh, I hope."

Perhaps my favorite of Watterson's transformational techniques was Calvin taking on full-blown alter egos: Safari Al, Spaceman Spiff, Captain Napalm, Tracer Bullet, Stupendous Man and — on one lone occasion — Wonga-Taa, King of Jungle. These personas lived in their own fantasy worlds, each drawn in a unique style. I was a particularly huge fan of Spaceman Spiff, because he allowed Watterson to draw gorgeous Martian canyons and mesas, tinged with reds, oranges and purples, as backdrops. The landscapes of these faraway worlds with their interstellar skylines were a beautiful addition to Watterson's geographic repertoire. Spiff also allowed Watterson to explore intergalactic storylines. As a fellow *Star Wars* kid, I thought that zooming across the interstellar void in my red spaceship and battling aliens with a frap-ray blaster was particularly appealing.

Even when Calvin is grounded on Earth, Watterson brings a sense of wonder to the natural world. There is a transportive quality to the snowy mornings and autumn afternoons he sketched out in black and white. You can feel this world wrapping itself around you and drawing you in — and the more you give in to Watterson's power of suggestion, the more fun you'll have.

In one panel in particular, Calvin and Hobbes are walking across a grassy meadow toward the forest on the far side. Watterson had to sketch only a few blades of grass and a lone tree in order to suggest the whole scene. Less artistically dexterous cartoonists would have to fill in every detail and every blade of grass. Next to nothing can be left to the imagination. This literalism distracts from the richness of the imaginative experience for the reader. The more you give the reader, the less their minds need to work. With Watterson's drawings you can't be complacent, you need to engage and imagine what is beyond the obvious. In this way, a casual walk across a meadow becomes an afternoon in the woods for the reader.

When he's not playing around the house or in the woods, Calvin's other main terrestrial sphere is his school, even though he studiously tries to avoid it. I don't blame him; it sounds like hell on earth. Calvin's not a good student and he's constantly being sent to the principal's office. He is bullied all the time, no one wants to hang out with him, the lunches his mom packs are horrifying and he's not good at organized sports. So, basically, everyone thinks he's a wimp who probably got dropped on his head as a small child. Even worse, he's not allowed to bring Hobbes with him to class, so he has no one who can share his imaginative life.

To relieve his boredom and bring some excitement into the classroom, Calvin either daydreams or tries to be the P. T. Barnum of show and tell. His presentations to the class fail to interest his fellow students, who just see a weird kid showing off what he considers to be cool stuff — dead flies he found on his windowsill, a yo-yo he retrieved from the afterlife or a poster he drew in 3-D Gore-o-rama. My favorite of these embarrassing episodes is when Calvin brings a lone snowflake into school. "I think we might all learn a lesson from how this utterly unique and exquisite crystal turns into an ordinary, boring molecule of water, just like every other one, when you bring it into the classroom," Calvin lectures. "And now, while the analogy sinks in, I'll be leaving you drips and going outside."

Because of episodes like this, Calvin's teacher, Miss Wormwood, is clearly one breakdown short of a heart attack. It's not hard to imagine the aging matron in the polka-dotted dress nipping at a bottle she's hidden in her desk to cope with Calvin. "I have a lot of sympathy for Miss Wormwood," Watterson admitted in his interview with *The Comics Journal*. "We see hints that she's waiting to retire, that she smokes too much, and that she takes a lot of medication. I think she seriously believes in the value of education, so needless to say, she's an unhappy person."

Wormwood's name is borrowed from the apprentice devil in C. S. Lewis's novel *The Screwtape Letters*. This devil's job is to keep his human charge on a course that will ultimately lead him away from God and into the awaiting arms of the Devil. The other authority figures at the school are portrayed with equal disdain. Principal Spittle and the gym teacher, Mr Lockjaw, both seem like they can't wait for Calvin to pass so they won't have to deal with him any more. Even Calvin's nameless classmates' main goal seems to be taunting and despising him. These characters represent censorship, they embody the idea of institutional control and loss of self. They seek to dampen

Calvin's imaginative life by trying to force him, an unusually shaped peg, into a square hole. Their goal is to lead him away from who he truly is — a mundane outcome for such an exceptional boy.

The only schoolmate who is glad that Calvin bothers to show up is Moe, if only so Moe can beat him up and steal his lunch money. A typically dunderheaded bully, Moe has a hacked-straw haircut that covers his eyes, and his speech appears as a bold, childish scrawl. "Moe is every jerk I've ever known," Watterson told *The Comics Journal*. "He's big, dumb, ugly and cruel. I remember school being full of idiots like Moe. I think they spawn on damp locker-room floors."

Even outside school, Calvin is afflicted by the constraints of authority and oppression. Rosalyn is his babysitter and occasional swim teacher. As Watterson put it to *The Comics Journal*, she is "the only person Calvin fears." Rosalyn made her first appearance on 15 May 1986 for a series of four strips, which Watterson thought might be the extent of her appearances. "I never expected to use her again," Watterson admitted in *Sunday Pages 1985–1995*. "Her ferocious personality surprised me, though, so she came back several times."

In her two initial interactions with Calvin she manages to contain and control him, first by locking him in the garage and then by threatening to call his parents. These would be her lone victories, because from then on, every time she'd show up — demanding more money for her pain and suffering from Calvin's parents, who have run out of other babysitting options — Calvin comes up with a new method of harassment. He locks her out of the house, tells her boyfriend that she's a "sadistic kid-hater" and takes her science homework hostage.

On the surface, this appears to be an obvious antagonist-protagonist set-up. "Rosalyn's relationship with Calvin is pretty one-dimensional," Watterson wrote in *Sunday Pages 1985–1995*, but I'm inclined to disagree. In a series of daily strips that ran in early September 1995, Rosalyn comes over for what will be her last time. The story starts as it normally does, with Calvin kicking and screaming over the thought of being left in Rosalyn's care. However, he strikes a different tone when she offers to make a deal with her pint-sized charge. If he doesn't give her any problems, then he can stay up half an hour past his bedtime and choose a game for them to play.

As expected, Calvin chooses Calvinball. Though this requires some explanation in the form of a song, Rosalyn soon picks up its nuance, cheerfully throwing herself into the madness of it all. For a brief moment, they are both racing across the panels in masks and enjoying the battle to outwit each other. It's the one time in the whole series that anyone other than Hobbes really understands Calvin and engages him on his own terms. If for that moment alone, Rosalyn is a truly rich character, capable of real empathy.

In the early years, Watterson tried to add other characters to his microverse, including a nameless doctor (inspired by Watterson's old friend David Bowe) and Pete the barber. Neither one stuck around for more than a few strips. In early 1988, Watterson introduced Calvin's Uncle Max, who came to visit the family. Calvin greets him with suspicion, warning him that he needs to beware of the "man-eating tiger" who will rip his lungs out. Later Uncle Max asks Calvin's mother, "Shouldn't he be playing with real friends?" She replies, "Oh, I think he will when he's ready. Didn't you ever have an imaginary friend?" Max morosely responds in the last frame, "Sometimes I think *all* my friends have been imaginary," sounding not unlike Charlie Brown.

Though the uncle appeared in only a handful of strips, he was clunky and unnatural. "[H]e didn't bring anything new to Calvin," Watterson wrote in the *Calvin and Hobbes Tenth Anniversary Book*. "It was also very awkward that Max could not address Calvin's parents by name, and this should have tipped me off that the strip was not designed for the parents to have outside adult relationships." West concurs: "Bill was burned by the uncle. Those strips lacked any spark and it's a dissonant note in the otherwise melodic flow of the strip." After he dispatched the uncle forevermore, Watterson decided that his cast of characters was complete. He wouldn't add others because he would say everything he needed to through the characters he already had.

There were other hiccups early on in the strip. For instance, Calvin and Hobbes go on a couple of camping trips with the Cub Scouts. "[T]he situation was always awkward," Watterson later wrote in the *Calvin and Hobbes Tenth Anniversary Book*. "Calvin and Hobbes need to be in their own world, so putting a troop of kids around them didn't provide much material. Eventually, I realized Calvin's not the kind of kid who would join a group anyway." So that was the end of the Cub Scout strips. Watterson enjoyed the outdoor stories so much, though, that he began sending Calvin's family on annual camping trips.

The camping trips were a great showcase for Calvin's dad. Despite the overwhelming indifference and cynicism of his wife and son, the father always optimistically touts the wonderful benefits of fresh air, a marked lack of conveniences and fishing in the rain. Despite this dauntless enthusiasm, he is alone in these beliefs, but it never seems to dim his wholehearted love of the great outdoors. These strips remind me of my own father, who was forever trying to get me to go fishing with him as a kid. Unfortunately, my idea of a good time didn't involve sitting out in sub-zero temperatures over a hole in the ice or giving up an early morning of reading comic books in bed to drive two hours into the middle of nowhere. (I now appreciate those shared adventures, because they brought my father and me together, united in time, place and space.)

Our fathers differed, however, when it came to the questions kids inevitably ask. When my dad didn't know the answers, he would plead ignorance, refer me to my mother or change the subject. Calvin's father can't admit his lack of knowledge, so he just makes stuff up. He gives all sorts of ridiculous explanations: Wind is caused by trees sneezing, babies are made from assembly kits bought at Sears, and ice floats because it wants to get warm so it moves up to the surface where it's closer to the sun. Given the far-fetched nature of his answers, it should be no surprise that Calvin has an active imagination and prefers to live in his own subjective reality.

No matter where I look in the strips, there is something to talk about. Ten years produces a lot of material. Rereading all of the strips took a three-day weekend and innumerable pots of coffee. Every new reading has led to new discoveries, new understandings and new questions scrawled into my notebook. At every step in this process, the more I learn, the less I feel I know. There is so much depth to *Calvin and Hobbes*, something that's sorely lacking in the funny pages. But that would all seem to be part of Watterson's master plan. "Behind the jokes, I try to talk about life in a serious way," he revealed in Lee Nordling's book *Your Career in Comics*. "I don't look at cartooning as just an entertainment. It's a rare privilege to be able to talk to hundreds of millions of people on a given day, and I don't want to squander that privilege with mindless chatter. There is an opportunity here to talk about real issues of life with sensitivity, warmth and humor."

This is one of the many reasons I wanted to speak with Watterson himself, to get a deeper sense of this philosophy he worked so hard at incorporating in his work. Frankly, I also want to find out the story behind "The Noodle Incident" to which Watterson alludes on several occasions but never explains. The reader understands that Calvin received the blame for it, though he claims that no one can prove he is guilty of it. What happened and why won't he tell us?

I had sent out innumerable letters and emails to anyone and everyone related to Watterson when I finally got word back from Bill's younger brother, Tom, who is an English teacher in Austin, Texas. Unfortunately, it wasn't the news I was hoping for. "Thank you for your kind words about my brother," he wrote in a brief email. "I choose to honor his work and his desire for privacy by declining all requests for interviews."

Argh. Dang rabbit! Curses to the trickster god Loki! I keep getting close, but not close enough. That Watterson is a one wascally wabbit. Though I'd been granted unparalleled access to his life from the colleagues, friends and peers with whom I had spoken thus far, moments like this still frustrated me. But as I was about learn, Watterson had thrown up these walls of privacy for more reasons than just the principles he espoused early in his career.

CHAPTER 6

Welcome to the Machine

When you're working under deadline for a newspaper and you have to constantly deliver new material, you have a tendency to feel that you're a fraud and that everything you've done till now has been luck. Or that you've given everything you have to give and now you're living on fumes, reputation and general fraudulence.

— Dave Barry, Pulitzer Prize-winning humorist

The 1980s was the decade of funny money. Big-name cartoonists were making big bucks by harnessing the selling power of their characters. Though cartoonists get paid a fee for every paper their strip appears in, and get paid advances and royalties on their books, these payments are traditionally split 50-50 between the artist and their syndicate. But there's a ceiling to what you can make in either medium — there are only so many papers in the world and the royalty rate on books is not particularly high. The real money for creators is in licensing, because it expands the cartoon's selling power into the mass market across mediums that have higher earning potential. At that time, cartoonists made around a 5–10 percent royalty on the wholesale price of any licensed item that featured one of their creations. Some cartoonists even got up-front bonuses for simply allowing a manufacturer to use their work.

Cartoon characters were slapped on everything from lunchboxes to T-shirts and transformed into everything from plush dolls and action figures to helium balloons and candles. So here's a math problem for the kids: If there were 255 million suction-cupped Garfield dolls sold over the course of the decade, how many small tropical islands was Jim Davis able to buy with the proceeds?

On top of all these licensed products, comic strip characters were even utilized as spokesmodels for major corporations. Cathy Guisewite's Cathy shilled for VISA and J. C. Penney; Schulz's characters advertised everything from Cheerios and A&W Root Beer to Ford automobiles, Coca-Cola and MetLife; and Jim Davis's Garfield endorsed everything from credit cards to cat food and chewing gum. Licensing comic creations was so lucrative that both Schulz and Davis ranked near the top of the *Forbes* wealthiest entertainers list in the late '80s.

This fad was nothing new; cartoon characters have been licensed since the early twentieth century. Percy Crosby's strip *Skippy* spawned a slew of merchandise, including dolls, toys and Skippy peanut butter (which continues to this day, long after the demise of the strip). Walt Kelly's *Pogo* inspired licensed spin-offs as varied as an album of the cartoonist's verses set to music and a series of giveaway figures packaged with Proctor and Gamble Soap. However, it was *Li'l Abner*, which ran from 1934–77, which may have been the first comic strip to really embrace licensing to the utmost degree. Over the strip's run, creator Al Capp allowed his characters to sell products as varied as Strunk chainsaws, Grape Nuts cereal, Head and Shoulders shampoo, Fruit of the Loom products and Kickapoo

Joy Juice, a soft drink based on a moonshine-like concoction drunk in the strip. Capp himself even endorsed Chesterfield cigarettes and Rheingold beer.

The thing that marketers and advertisers realized early on was that cartoon characters are inherently merchandisable and infinitely exploitable. They are eternally youthful, never talk back and can have broad appeal. Syndicates and cartoonists realized this, too, which is why United had been so keen to have Watterson incorporate the Robotman character into *Calvin and Hobbes*. Another example of this is *Garfield*. Jim Davis always hoped that *Garfield* would yield a licensing bonanza. Three years after the strip debuted, Davis founded Paws, Inc., a separate licensing arm of his growing empire that would create and oversee new business ventures based on the fat feline. Within a year, Davis had seven *Garfield* collections on the *New York Times* best-seller list, and by 2004, *Garfield* products ranging from slot machines to theme cruises were raking in between 750 million and one billion dollars a year across 111 countries.

Today *Garfield* is the most widely read strip in the world, with Paws, Inc. estimating that around 260 million people read it every day (that is almost 4 percent of the globe's population, for those of you looking for a calculator). And there is no end to the merchandise available; just go online to the furry feline's official website where you'll be boggled by the hundreds of options available. I have spent a few minutes on the site just to take a quick survey of the empire, but it was too overwhelming. And no, I did not buy a mug from the Fat Cat Coffeehouse that proclaims, "The eyelids go up when the coffee goes down," even though it does, technically, speak to me.

I'm not ashamed to say that, growing up, I was a fan of *Garfield* and there are still a couple of my favorite strips on my mother's fridge. However, unlike *Calvin and Hobbes* or *The Far Side*, *Garfield* stopped being funny to me at some point. I can't remember when it happened, but I remember the change was sudden. It was one of those moments as a teenager when you're about to put on a piece of clothing (in my case, anything with a Bugle Boy label) or listening to a record (something by DJ Jazzy Jeff and the Fresh Prince, probably) and you suddenly think, "This isn't me anymore." Then you think, "I can't believe this was *ever* me!" Garfield was dead to me after that epiphany. I still nostalgically chuckle at the yellowed strips hanging in the kitchen of my childhood home, but I've never reread any of the old collections. I got the joke; now there's nothing more to laugh about.

Regardless of how I feel about the strip, Garfield is inarguably one of the most recognizable cartoon characters in the world. He is certainly right up there with Mickey Mouse, Superman and Homer Simpson. I wanted to hear why Davis chose to embrace licensing and merchandising with such exaggerated abandon. I tracked him down in Muncie, Indiana, where he and more than 60 Paws staffers oversee the orange-and-black-striped empire. Davis did not have time for a phone interview, but he graciously answered my questions by email, happily admitting his appreciation for Watterson. "*Calvin and Hobbes* is one of my favorite strips of all time," he wrote. "Talk about imagination! The strip was a masterpiece."

"I still consider the comic strip the most important thing I do," he wrote in response to my questions about his feelings on licensing. "I didn't put the pen to paper when I first drew Garfield thinking, "Oh, now I'm going to create a licensing empire." It just evolved thanks to the books and the TV shows." He was also quick to point out — perhaps a little defensively — that he considers the strip and the licensing of it to be two different entities. "I've learned a lot about Garfield from working on plush and in animation," he said in his email. "I get to see more sides of his personality working with him in other mediums. So for me, it's helped the feature."

Considering that over the years there have been thousands of different *Garfield* items, you have to wonder if there has ever been an offer that he turned down. Though I did not get an answer to that question, Davis did tell me that he thought that toilet seats were the weirdest licensing offer he did get. "Litter boxes made sense to me, but toilet seats . . . that was a bit of a stretch," he wrote, though it didn't turn out to be too much of a stretch. "We did the product," he continued. "They convinced me that humor can and should be carried into the bathroom."

Davis has never hidden the fact that he wanted to create a character with widespread appeal and merchandising potential. He had seen the success of Snoopy as a licensed character and he used the *Peanuts* empire as a blueprint, because it was Schulz who had set the bar. By the time Schulz retired, the *Peanuts* franchise earned an estimated one billion dollars a year, with Schulz himself taking home about 30 to 40 million dollars annually. This wasn't, erm, peanuts by anyone's standards and it made syndicates and cartoonists realize how much more money they could be milking from their cartoon properties.

It was quickly apparent to everyone at Universal that *Calvin and Hobbes* was a huge commercial hit and they might be able to start making some of that crazy funny money. There was little stopping them. Watterson's original contract with Universal had the syndicate controlling ancillary rights and splitting the revenues with the artist. This was a standard deal for freshman cartoonists, most of whom were more than happy to have their syndicate seek additional sources of income from their work. This meant that the syndicate would try to capitalize on successful derivative merchandise — Hobbes dolls, Spaceman Spiff Underoos, Stupendous Man T-shirts, a Saturday morning TV series, whatever.

However, unlike almost all of his peers, Watterson was not keen on exploiting his creations. "Licensing couldn't have been further from his mind when he was trying to make his little world emerge," Rich West explained to me. "He wasn't sitting next to his drawing board and rubbing his hands together in anticipation of all the money he could make." In fact, the avalanche of commercial interest blindsided the modest young artist. His first reaction was to just say no as he sat back and considered the ramifications of licensing. "Bill's not one of these people who says, "I want the money and I want the fame and I want the attention,"" West revealed. "All he wanted to do was to draw the strip as best as he could. If he was going to be rewarded for that, then that was great, but that wasn't ever the goal. He simply wanted to be able to pay his bills by being able to draw."

Watterson's modest vision of success was puzzling to Universal, whose other artists were pestering them for the kinds of offers that Watterson was reflexively turning down. After all, who doesn't want to be successful and earn a boatload of money? Well, Watterson didn't. Everyone at Universal quickly realized that Watterson's dream was vastly different and that this new-found fame was more like a nightmare to him. Watterson wasn't just uncomfortable with his characters becoming ubiquitous; he was worried about becoming ubiquitous himself. Despite the fact that he had told Salem that he didn't want to do any further interviews after his negative experience with the *Los Angeles Times* interviewer, Watterson agreed to sit down with the *Plain Dealer* in the summer of 1987. Though the interviewer probably went to get a piece on Watterson's happiness with his success, he got something completely different — a full-on rant that was Watterson's manifesto against celebrity. The resulting article ran in the *Plain Dealer* magazine of 30 August 1987 and bore the front-page headline "The Angry Artist Behind Lovable Calvin and Hobbes."

The writer meets up with Watterson at his "small," "cramped" and "difficult to find" house in Hudson, where the artist is hanging out with his wife and three cats, Pumpernickel, Sprite and Juniper Boots. Watterson answers the door wearing large-framed glasses and his work outfit, "yellow high-top sneakers, purple socks, yellow slacks, a striped shirt and thin blue belt," as well as red, green and purple Swatch. Though he has a Marine-length buzz cut, his moustache is profuse, as is his ability to laugh over the course of what is not such a laughable discussion.

"I know most people dream of being famous or being a celebrity," Watterson confided to sports editor Gene Williams, who conducted the interview. "The attention is thought to be gratifying, or ego-building or something. I've found it to be a nuisance all the way around. There's very little of it that I enjoy." Apparently, that celebrity was an unwanted yoke of oppression. "You become a cartoonist all your life, all day," he continued. "It's no longer a job. You are defined by your work. You suddenly have no private time. You cannot be a husband to your wife, you are still a celebrity cartoonist . . . I find that aggravating. If you can't have a personal life, it really seems to me to be a sacrifice."

"As a culture, we embrace people for no reason other than the fact that they have a job that puts them in a position of recognizability," Watterson aggressively opined. "People who have no other virtues necessarily are somehow made into these things that we devour . . . There's something very strange about our fascination with other people's lives that I don't think is entirely healthy."

This was Watterson's strongest statement to date on his aversion for the recognition that had accompanied the rise of *Calvin and Hobbes*. Though he had discussed his discomfort with autograph seekers and being recognized in public before, this last conversation really finds him lashing out at the construct of celebrity. Even then, he recognized that his stance might be misunderstood. "[P]eople think I'm either a grouch," he declared, "or that I somehow think myself better than other people, and I'm just not willing to expose myself to the unwashed masses. Neither is the case. It's just that I want to have my own life, too."

"As part of this devouring process," he continued, "people love to have you, and then they use you up and there's nothing left. They're not interested anymore. It's a cyclical thing." Watterson was especially afraid of this devouring because of the negative effect it could have on the sustainability of his work. "There are trends where there is a hot strip and then people don't care anymore," he opined. "A certain amount of that is inevitable. But I'd like to control it if I can."

His final comment is the one that would prove to be most prophetic. "[W]hy start compromising values now?" he asked Williams. "Why tamper with what's important to me? The whole fun of doing this is I beat the odds. I beat the system. I get to do what I want, the way I want to do it. There's no point in buckling under now after I've made it."

He didn't buckle either. Over the next year, as the strip continued to gain a larger readership in more papers, Watterson staunchly refused to play the game, even though Salem remembers being flooded with offers. Watterson may not have arrived at a definitive answer regarding how he was to proceed; pending the answer, he enacted a total moratorium on promotion and merchandising. "He has a tendency to state things emphatically when he's trying to prove it to himself," West says now. "It's not that he starts out with exceedingly strongly held beliefs, he's just trying clarify things in his own mind and work through them."

Needless to say, everyone at the syndicate was eager to monetize the strip and Watterson's internal debates were a frustrating turn of events for the licensing department. Since Universal was contractually and legally allowed to pursue these business opportunities, this led to a relationship that Salem diplomatically called "negative, at times." However, the syndicate knew that licensing unapproved by Watterson would seriously antagonize their new-found talent. And pushed too far, Watterson might decide to break his contract and walk away. "We were lucky that he didn't call one day and say, "I quit,"" Salem admits now.

Given that the strip would be the driving advertisement for the merchandise, everyone felt that it was best to get Watterson on board, since it was hard to imagine someone other than Watterson drawing and writing *Calvin and Hobbes*. This was not your run-of-the-mill, gag-a-day strip with average artwork that anyone could do. The syndicate knew that *Calvin and Hobbes* grew out of Watterson and that trying to separate the two from one another would be disastrous, probably signaling the strip's death knell.

There was also a hope that Watterson would cave in, in light of the propositions, which were becoming obscenely huge. Finally, after two years of intense discussion and heated argument, Watterson relented by allowing a modest 16-month calendar to be made for 1988–9. Considering some of the other offers that were made, allowing this one piece of merchandise was by no means a cash grab; this was merely Watterson putting a toe in the water. The calendar sold well and Watterson even produced another for the following year, but it was not the birth of the licensing juggernaut that Universal was hoping for.

This initial experience was clearly weighing on his mind when Watterson visited Ohio State University on 25 August 1988 to celebrate *Pogo* cartoonist Walt Kelly's 75th birthday. Surprisingly, curator Lucy Caswell was able to convince Watterson to take some time away from his drawing board to give a speech highlighting his appreciation for Kelly's work, though he did it with the strict stipulation that no photos could be taken and he would give no interviews. Watterson spent the speech praising Kelly until the very end, when he suddenly announced, "I cannot resist going off on two nasty tangents of my own, since it is not often I have a large group of people more or less held captive before me."

"[T]he comic world is much more fragile than most people realize," Watterson told the audience. "[W]onderful, lifelike characters are easily corrupted and cheapened by having them appear on every drugstore shelf and rack." Though he admitted to seeing a couple of *Pogo* products over the years, Watterson expressed his happiness that Kelly had never done much in the way of licensing and in that refusal had set a new, mostly ignored, precedent for cartoonists. "Several fine strips have turned themselves into shameless advertisements for products," Watterson disgustedly declared, before moving on to talk about his worries about the shrinking size of the comics section.

For a guy who didn't get out of the house that much, this was a strong statement. However, it paled in comparison to his next public appearance, at the Festival of Cartoon Art the following year (though Caswell remembers him returning to the campus once in the interim to talk to a journalism class she was teaching). Every three years, OSU hosts a weekend-long celebration that brings together academics, cartoonists and their fans to discuss the history and the craft of cartooning. Watterson, perhaps buoyed by his previous talk, agreed to give a speech, though this would be nothing but (as he might put it) "nasty tangents."

When Watterson took the stage on 27 October 1989, the audience was buzzing. Here was one of cartooning's biggest and most reserved stars, ready to deliver what promised to be an exciting speech. It turned out to be very exciting, but not in that "Oh my God, I just hooked up with Jessica Biel" sort of way. Instead, it was more like an "Oh my God, a freakish monster is tearing my camping buddies to shreds" moment. Entitled "The cheapening of the comics," Watterson's speech started out on a harsh tangent and did not stop.

The speech took exception to everything and everyone — no one was left unscathed. One of the first shots Watterson fired was at syndicates for encouraging young artists to work on legend strips, rather than on their own new material. For their part, the syndicates were always afraid that losing an older, proven strip would lead to the loss of a spot on the comics page to a rival syndicate. "Consequently, the comics pages are full of dead wood," Watterson told the crowd. "Strips that had some relevance to the world during the Depression are now being continued by baby boomers, and the results are embarrassing."

Though he took pains not to name any strips in particular, Chic Young's *Blondie* is probably one of the strips set ablaze by Watterson's wrath. Young created the strip in 1930 and worked on it until his death in 1973, at which point his son, Dean, took over the strip. The younger Young also employed a number of other cartoonists to help him with the art, which was something else that Watterson took issue with, dubbing these cartoonists "official plagiarists." In keeping with this, Watterson proposed the following question to his audience: "Suppose you're a painter and you go to an art gallery to see if they'll represent you. They look at your work and shake their heads. But, since you show some basic familiarity with a paintbrush, they ask if you'd like to continue Rembrandt's work. After all, you can paint. Rembrandt's dead, and some buyers would rather have a Rembrandt forgery than no Rembrandt at all. It's an absurd scenario, but this is what goes on in comic-strip syndication."

"If someone wants to be a cartoonist, let's see him develop his own strip instead of taking over the duties of someone else's," Watterson told the crowd. "We've got too many comic-strip corpses being propped up and passed for living by new cartoonists who ought to be doing something of their own. If a cartoonist isn't good enough to make it on his own work, he has no business being in the newspaper."

If the audience thought that that was the end of Watterson's issues, they had only heard the beginning. He rebuked the syndicates again, this time for making merchandising of cartoons such a cornerstone of their business models — although, he quickly pointed out, "most cartoonists are happy to sell out." He did allow that he wasn't against all licensing and there were ways to tastefully and respectfully license a strip, but "it's very rarely done that way." Considering the kind of money a cartoonist could earn from these deals, "it's not surprising many cartoonists are as eager as the syndicates for easy millions, and are willing to sacrifice the heart and soul of the strip to get it."

Since licensing programs usually require the oversight of someone other than the cartoonist, separate staffs are hired to help with these operations. Watterson felt that this led to a too-many-cooks-in-the-kitchen mentality, as the cartoonist tries to please everyone. "Once a lot of money and jobs are riding on the status quo, it gets harder to push the experiments and new directions that keep a strip vital," Watterson argued. "Characters lose their believability as they start endorsing major companies and lend their faces to bed sheets and boxer shorts. The appealing innocence and sincerity of cartoon characters is corrupted when they use those qualities to peddle products. One starts to question whether characters say things because they mean it or because their sentiments sell T-shirts and greeting cards."

Near the end of his lengthy excoriation, Watterson finally got to his mission statement. It is perhaps his most concise public testimony concerning his career and motivations I read during the entire research for this book. "I consider it a great privilege to be a cartoonist," he professed to the crowd. "I love my work, and I am grateful for the incredible forum I have to express my thoughts. People give me their attention for a few seconds every day, and I take that as an honor and a responsibility. I try to give readers the best strip I'm capable of doing. I look at cartoons as an art, as a form of personal expression. That's why I don't hire assistants, why I write and draw every line myself, why I draw and paint special art for each of my books, and why I refuse to dilute or corrupt the strip's message with merchandising. I want to draw cartoons, not supervise a factory. I had a lot of fun as a kid reading comics, and now I'm in the position where I can return some of that fun."

Watterson ended with a call to arms: "Newspapers can do better. Syndicates can do better. Cartoonists can do better. The business interests, in the name of efficiency, mass marketability, and profit, profit, profit are catering to the lowest common denominator of readership and are keeping this art form from growing. There will always be mediocre comic strips, but we have lost much of the potential for anything else." According to witnesses, he took no questions before walking off stage and taking a seat at the back of the shocked and confused audience.

Dave Coverly, who draws the one-panel gag strip *Speed Bump*, was there that day. He was an aspiring cartoonist then and wasn't syndicated yet, so the weekend was a chance for him to mingle with his heroes. I caught up with Coverly by phone to talk about his memories of what he calls a "semi-inspiring, semi-cringe-worthy" experience. "For us young cartoonists, it was like, "Yeah, that's what we think,"" Coverly admitted. "But you're surrounded by some of the dinosaurs he was talking about, so you're going, "Ummm . . . what am I supposed to do?""

The next morning Mort Walker got up in front of the same audience. "I'm one of those old dinosaurs Bill Watterson was talk-ing about," he joked, before launching into a defense of cartooning and the cartoon business model. Walker is what you could call a classic cartoonist. His two strips, *Beetle Bailey* and *Hi and Lois*, are simply drawn and use a gag-a-day writing style. There are no longer story arcs, and strips steer clear of any controversial subject matter. Though Walker wasn't mentioned by name, it's a good bet that Watterson wasn't a fan.

To this day, Walker works out of his Connecticut studio, which has walls overcrowded with art given to him by a myriad of cartoonists. I tracked him down there one day in late 2008 and he opened up to me about his OSU experience. "Watterson had a tremendous amount of talent," Walker told me at the top of our conversation. "And if you read his work, you'd think he'd be a friendly, nice guy with a lot of fun in him. Frankly, after that speech I was disappointed."

Walker's own rebuttal speech steered far clear of any controversy, much like his work. "I want to appeal to the broadest readership I can," Walker admitted without pretense. "A lot of people feel like that's copping out; I'm sure Trudeau does. They think it's good to shake up the public and challenge their beliefs." After Walker gave his rebuttal, he tried to go talk to Watterson, who lingered in the back of the auditorium, but, as he remembers it, members of Watterson's syndicate kept him and everyone else away. The two men have never talked since.

Somewhat ironically, before seeing him at OSU, Walker had written Watterson on a couple of occasions to compliment him on some strips that had struck his fancy. "Usually when I write a guy a fan letter I get an original to hang on my wall," Walker told me. "But he didn't even write back. I guess he's just the opposite of the kind of person that I am. I'm gregarious and like to be around people. I like to take compliments."

As our conversation was coming to a close, Walker confessed to me, "I hate myself for talking to you the way I am, because I never malign another cartoonist. We're all friends, even though we're competitors. We play golf together and love each other's company." So what would he say to Watterson if he had the chance? "Come on over, let's talk. We'll go out to lunch and have a drink."

Though she wasn't in the audience that day, *For Better or For Worse* creator Lynn Johnston remembers the speech and its aftermath. "It was not well received amongst cartoonists," is how she diplomatically put it with a chuckle. Watterson was not prepared for the backlash and Johnston believes that this pushed him into self-imposed exile from his peers on a wider scale. "He never really did come back to us," Johnston admitted. "He never did join in any other reindeer games. He went back to his home, hunkered down and pulled down the shutters."

Watterson never again spoke publicly to his peers, but over the next several years he expounded on his distaste for licensing in the few interviews he did grant and in a few essays. In his foreword to the George Herriman collection, *The Komplete Kolor Krazy Kat*, Watterson took a few minutes off from praising the cartoonist to turn his poison quill back at the licensing beast. "The comics have become big business, and they play it safe," he wrote. "They shamelessly pander to the results of reader surveys, and are produced by virtual factories, ready-made for the inevitable T-shirts, dolls, greeting cards, and television specials. Licensing is where the money is, and we seem to have forgotten that a comic strip can be something more than a launch pad for a glut of derivative products. When the comic strip is not exploited, the medium can be a vehicle for beautiful artwork and serious, intelligent expression."

When Rich West interviewed him for *The Comics Journal* in 1989, Watterson firmly stated that he felt that licensing was "inconsistent" with his vision for the strip. He didn't condemn across the board, however, because he felt that one-panel gag strips maintained their integrity when transferred amongst mediums. Readers never lost their knowledge of the strip's larger universe when each joke is self-contained, but that wasn't the case with his work. "It has a punch line, but the strip is about more than that," Watterson told his friend. "The humor is situational, and often episodic. It relies on conversation, and the development of personalities and relationships. These aren't concerns you can wrap up neatly in a clever little saying for people to send each other or to hang up on their walls. To explore character, you need lots of time and space. Notepads and coffee mugs just aren't appropriate vehicles for what I'm trying to do here. I'm not interested in removing all the subtlety from my work to condense it for a product."

"I'm convinced that licensing would sell out the soul of *Calvin and Hobbes*," he continued later. "The world of a comic strip is much more fragile than most people realize. Once you've given up its integrity, that's it. I want to make sure that never happens. Instead of asking what's wrong with rampant commercialism, we ought to be asking, "What justifies it?" Popular art does not have to pander to the lowest level of intelligence and taste."

This sentiment came up in a series of *Calvin and Hobbes* strips that ran in mid-1992. "If you want to influence people, **popular** art is the way to go," Calvin lectures as he works a piece of clay. "Mass market commercial art is the future. Besides, it's the only way to make serious money and that's what's important about being an artist." Hobbes asks, "So what kind of sculpture are you making?" "Please!" Calvin retorts. "It's not "sculpture." It's "collectible figurines."" In the next day's strip he continues ranting: "[T]he problem with fine art is that it's supposed to express original truths. But who likes originality and truth?! Nobody! Life's hard enough without it! Only an idiot would **pay** for it! But **popular** art knows the customer is always right! People want **more** of what they already **know** they like, so popular art gives it to 'em!"

Calvin and Hobbes often discussed, dissected and dissed the art world, which, Watterson once wrote, "attracts its share of pretentious blowhards." These discourses usually happened in the snowman strips. In one such episode, Calvin is building a snowman, despite Hobbes's reminder that the one he made the day before had already melted. "I'm taking advantage of my medium's impermanence," Calvin boasts. "This sculpture is about transience. As this figure melts, it invites the viewer to contemplate the evanescence of life. This piece speaks to the horror of our own mortality."

In another, Calvin takes in a neighbor's creation: "Look at that kid's snowman! What a pathetic cliché! Am I supposed to identify with this complacent moron and his shovel?? This snowman says nothing about the human condition! Is this all the kid has to say about contemporary suburban life?!" In a third, from 10 January 1993, Calvin rants: "Art is dead! There's nothing left to say. Style is exhausted and content is pointless. Art has no purpose. All that's left is commodity marketing."

Commodity marketing was clearly a repugnant idea to Watterson and in the interview with *The Comics Journal* he took particular offense at the idea of a Hobbes doll. "A doll only cashes in on the recognizability of the character," he told West. "Products like that take the character out of the world for which he was intended. If you stick thirty Hobbes dolls on a drugstore shelf, you're no longer talking about a character I created. At that point, you've transformed him into just another overpriced knick-knack. I have no interest in turning my characters into commodities. If I'd wanted to sell plush garbage, I'd have gone to work as a carnie."

"The idea of a Hobbes doll is especially noxious, because the intrigue of Hobbes is that he may or may not be a real tiger," he railed. "The strip deliberately sets up two versions of reality without committing itself to either one. If I'm not going to answer the question of who or what Hobbes is, I'm certainly not going to let [stuffed toy manufacturer] Dakin answer it. It makes no sense to allow someone to make Hobbes into a stuffed toy for real, and deprive the strip of an element of its magic."

Brian Walker passed on a story that Lee Salem had told him about Watterson's hardcore distaste for the Hobbes doll idea. Apparently, a plush-toy manufacturer sent Watterson a box of Hobbes dolls unannounced when he was living in New Mexico. As the story goes, Watterson took the dolls into the backyard and torched them all without a second thought, before calling Salem to berate him for giving the company his address. Another apocryphal myth from this period that I heard from several people, including Patrick Oliphant, was that the president of Universal showed up on Watterson's doorstep with a million-dollar offer to have a Hobbes doll made. "That never happened," Salem quickly denied, though he didn't refute that there were numerous, extended conversations on the topic. "We had strenuous discussions to the point of arguments with him, but there were never any concrete offers like that put on the table."

"Would it really have been so bad to let all us kids have a Hobbes doll?" *Pearls Before Swine* creator Stephan Pastis asked, when I raised the idea of Watterson's licensing some toys. "I'm not saying do MetLife, but would it really have hurt to have a Hobbes stuffed animal?" *Bone*'s Jeff Smith added when we talked, "I would personally have loved to have a Hobbes toy. But it's Watterson's character; he can do whatever he wants. My rule is if it's something I would want, I will do it. I want a toy of Bone, and I have them. And anyone who wants one can get one, too."

A lot of cartoonists I spoke with said they appreciated seeing their fans personally interacting with their creations. Berke Breathed told me people still drag out their bruised and battered Opus dolls when he does signings. "To one's fans, the toys aren't junk at all," he explained to me. "But if Watterson didn't want to see his work in plush dolls, jolly good. Junk is junk. Although, it's an opportunity to extend their affection for your work into something more tangible in their lives: a figure on their work desk that will make them smile. To deny them that — to tell them that their wish for the little vinyl figure is corrupt — is an abstract bit of selfishness maybe."

In the absence of any official merchandise, a number of contraband products flooded the market. There was a huge demand for *Calvin and Hobbes* products, and if you go online you can still find everything from bootlegged hats and pendants to pins, watches and light-switch covers. However, the most memorable bootleg item began showing up in the early '90s on the back windows of cars. It's a decal of Calvin, with a devilish grin on his face, pissing — oftentimes on a car manufacturer's logo or the car number of a NASCAR driver. One can only imagine the disgust Watterson feels when he drives by one of these co-opted creations. He's probably pretty, well, pissed.

Calvin and Hobbes were also used on bootleg T-shirts, many of them made by college students and rejiggered to include references to drinking and drugging. Though Watterson's own college strips involved a fair amount of drinking and even a few drug references, the unauthorized shirts clearly deviated from his worldview for *Calvin and Hobbes*. I have a semi-vivid college memory — blurred by one vice or the other — of being in a concert parking lot and seeing one of these contraband shirts mixed in amongst the Phish tie-dyes and the prismatic *Dark Side of the Moon* tees. The shirt borrowed the images of Calvin and Hobbes dancing to classical music cranked up to 78 rpm in the wee hours of the morning ("Illustrations from this strip were popular for copyright violations," Watterson bitterly quipped in *The Calvin and Hobbes Tenth Anniversary Book*). Except in this version, the pair is dancing around to the sonic stylings of the Grateful Dead. I am not sure Calvin would have grown up to be a Deadhead — I always saw him as more of a Beatles guy — but it's still funny to think of him cutting the rug to "Sugar Magnolia."

There was one lone licensed T-shirt that was produced. In 1991 the Smithsonian and OSU put together an exhibit entitled "Great American Comics: 100 Years of Cartoon Art." Watterson allowed his Sunday strip of Calvin making faces for the camera to be used on a T-shirt promoting the show, but he never allowed that again. Around that same time, the contraband T-shirt issue became so problematic that Tom Thornton (who worked at Watterson's book publisher, Andrews and McMeel) and Lee Salem went to visit Watterson to discuss it. To make their point, they laid out a dozen bootleg *Calvin and Hobbes* T-shirts on Watterson's living-room table. The shirts had been gathered all over the country as a representative, but small, sample of the illegal products being made. According to Salem, the businessmen told Watterson that the best way to monitor these types of copyright infringements was to legitimately license his work. That way, there would be a separate company with a vested interest in cracking down on illegal merchandise and Watterson wouldn't have to personally sheriff his creations. The two men even offered to direct all the profits from the legitimate products into a fund that would be set up to save tigers worldwide. With little discussion, Watterson refused.

So, since no one was specifically tasked with monitoring potential copyright infringement, most of the bootleg tees made it under the radar without prosecution and still pop up on eBay occasionally. However, there was one big crackdown on Aaron Unger, an LA-based wholesaler, who was sued for using *Calvin and Hobbes* logos and images in the early '90s. Ultimately, he ended up having to pay $737,000 in damages to Universal Press Syndicate. Other than that one instance, I could not find further evidence of any other lawsuits brought against any manufacturers, though there were certainly a number of cease-and-desist letters sent out by the Universal legal team.

Whether they wanted to plaster them on T-shirts or turn them into dolls, people wanted to transform Calvin and Hobbes into larger-than-life stars. George Lucas, Jim Henson and Steven Spielberg all courted Watterson at different times in the late '80s, hoping to take his creation off the page and onto the screen. Salem remembers Spielberg's people calling not once, but twice, which was probably a first for them. The editor dutifully phoned Watterson and passed along what he thought was exciting news, but Bill's response was as far from enthusiastic as you can get. "Why would I want to talk to Steven Spielberg?" he asked Salem, before refusing to call the director back. When George Lucas invited him out to Skywalker Ranch, he turned down that offer as well.

"I wouldn't have hesitated, because they were giants in their fields," Rich West told me after I recounted the "dissing Spielberg" story. "It would be interesting, something to tell the grandkids about." Breathed has always been flabbergasted by this particular incident, because he spent five years developing an Opus film at Miramax, which he described as the "antithesis of a good experience." As of this writing, there is no film on the horizon, because ultimately Breathed felt as if he would have to give up control in order to get the film made, something he was unprepared to do. However, he thinks Watterson would have had more leverage at the height of his fame. "Watterson would've been able to have control of a 100-million-dollar movie," he theorized. "He would've been able to draw every frame if he wanted to. And he would have had a better shot of a great movie made from his strip than anyone else, but that doesn't mean it would've been good. I guess he didn't think it would be worth the risk."

None of this was of any interest to Watterson, though. He didn't want a movie, he didn't want T-shirts and he didn't want dolls. He just wanted to create *Calvin and Hobbes*. Every time he had to turn down an offer and explain himself, it took a little more out of him. After waging this war for almost five years, it was distracting him from his work and making the work itself less enjoyable.

What would be Watterson's last public appearance took place in the midst of all this turmoil. It was at his alma mater, Kenyon College, on 20 May 1990, where he was the chosen commencement speaker. He gave a speech, "Some thoughts on the real world by one who glimpsed it and fled," which dealt mostly with the story of painting the Sistine Chapel on his dorm-room ceiling, but still managed to touch on the issue of licensing his work.

"Selling out is usually more a matter of buying in," he told the assembled graduates. "Sell out, and you're really buying into someone else's system of values, rules and rewards. The so-called "opportunity" I faced would have meant giving up my individual voice for that of a money-grubbing corporation. It would have meant my purpose in writing was to sell things, not say things. My pride in craft would be sacrificed to the efficiency of mass production and the work of assistants. Authorship would become committee decision. Creativity would become work for pay. Art would turn into commerce. In short, money was supposed to supply all the meaning I'd need. What the syndicate wanted to do, in other words, was turn my comic strip into everything calculated, empty and robotic that I hated about my old job. They would turn my characters into television hucksters and T-shirt sloganeers and deprive me of characters that actually expressed my own thoughts."

Watterson's former art professor, Martin Garhart, acting as "a chaperone and a bodyguard," remembers talking with Watterson that day. They were walking across the parking lot after the commencement; Watterson was clearly in a reflective mood and the concept of integrity came up. "Integrity is a really interesting word to try to handle," Garhart mused to me. "But on one level, it's just doing what you say you'll do and being honest with yourself." He remembers being proud of his former student, telling him, "I can talk about integrity, but no one has ever offered me multi-million dollars to test it. But you've had that offer and you said no. I really admire that." Watterson replied, "Enough is enough, and I have enough." It was a short and simple declaration, but it encapsulated Watterson's resistance to licensing and celebrity. Ultimately, this unorthodox worldview would power the cataclysm that was lurking in the next panel of his life.

CHAPTER 7

This is How You Disappear

Calvin's the square peg in the round hole. He will not let society conform him or water him down. He doesn't always win, but he never gives it up. That's the part of *Calvin and Hobbes* that means so much to me. And who doesn't like drawings of spaceships and dinosaurs? Those are both very high on the Neato Scale.

— Jeff Smith, creator of *Bone*

The 5 January 1989 *Calvin and Hobbes* shows the pair walking across a spare winter landscape. "What do you think is the best way to get what you want?" Calvin asks Hobbes. "Is it better to hold fast and never back down, or to compromise?" Hobbes stops to ponder for a second before responding, "I suppose it's best to hold fast when you can, and compromise when you need to." As the characters amble away towards the far side of the last frame, Calvin grumbles, "That's a lot more mature than I think I care to be."

"There were some very tough days in that period," Salem admitted to me. "I regret to say that some of our discussions impacted his creative process and you can see those dark strains in the strip." Watterson singled out several strips in particular in *The Calvin and*

Hobbes Tenth Anniversary Book. In one, Calvin only sees his world in black and white, just like the syndicate accused Watterson of doing. It ends with Calvin defiantly yelling at his father, "Sometimes that's the way things are!" In another strip Calvin rants, "I stand **firm** in my belief of what's right! I **refuse** to compromise my principles!" His mother makes him take a bath anyway, causing Calvin to grumble, "I don't **need** to compromise my principles, because they don't have the slightest bearing on what happens to me anyway."

The irony of this was lost on no one at the syndicate. Watterson was using the very medium he was fighting for to argue his case. Thankfully, most readers were oblivious to the brutal back-and-forth that was going on behind the scenes and creeping into the panels of the strip. *Calvin and Hobbes* topped endless newspaper reader polls for favorite comic strip and Universal received large amounts of fan mail for their artist. His peers either didn't notice — or didn't care about — the darkness either. Watterson won the Harvey Award for "Best Syndicated Comic Strip" seven years in a row from 1990–6. In all those years he never once showed up to claim his award.

He did, however, show up when it was time to argue with Universal. Though Salem and others I spoke with were understandably hesitant to discuss the finer points of their business dealings with Watterson, they were able to confirm a few points. In early 1991, Watterson and Universal's battle over the cartoonist's contract intensified. Watterson wanted to control his creation and ensure that no licensing ever happened. Without this assurance he was going to walk away from his career. Everyone in the room knew that this wasn't a bluff — it was either his way or no way at all. "There were a lot of conversations on our end about what our purpose was as a syndicate," Salem admitted. "Ultimately, we decided that if we're going to be in the business of attracting and cultivating talent, then the last thing we wanted to do is have the reputation of beating up one of the great stars of the past two decades."

So, after six years of bitter disputes, Universal caved in and relinquished the full ownership of the strip to Watterson. This meant that there would be no merchandise of any kind and that Universal was giving up millions of dollars in potential revenue. "If Bill had just let us license *Calvin and Hobbes*, you wouldn't be talking to me today," Salem quipped. "You'd be tracking me down on a beach in the Bahamas." An entirely new contract between Watterson and Universal was drawn up, memorializing the shift of ownership and control. It must have hurt the syndicate to sign away such a promising revenue stream. No one would discuss the details of this new arrangement with me, though they acknowledged that it ensured that Watterson finally controlled his characters and it brought Watterson back from what surely would have been the sudden demise of *Calvin and Hobbes*. They hoped that the new arrangement would placate Watterson enough that he would continue to draw *Calvin and Hobbes* for years to come and without interruption.

Their hopes were dashed when this contractual victory wasn't enough for Watterson. He also demanded two nine-month sabbaticals, the first one to take place immediately. To put this into perspective, most cartoonists don't ever get to take vacations from their readers. If they want to take time off, they have to draw enough strips in advance to cover their absence, so that readers will always have a new strip every day. Artists don't just put their strips into reruns for a couple of weeks every August so they can go sit on a beach somewhere. They always had to be producing. The exceptions to this rule were Garry Trudeau and Gary Larson. Trudeau had actually taken several sabbaticals during his career, including one that lasted almost two years when he brought *Doonesbury* to Broadway. However, these cartoonists were only allowed to take these breaks because of their enormous successes and loyal readers.

Realizing that they didn't have a choice, Universal gave Watterson his sabbatical, and on 5 May 1991, *Calvin and Hobbes* went into reruns. In prepared comments from the syndicate, Watterson playfully told his readers, "The strip requires a great deal of research and I need to do more interplanetary exploration and paleontology work before I continue." Some papers were so saddened by the temporary absence of new material that they ran countdown clocks to let readers know how many days they had left before they would get a new dose of their favorite strip.

For Watterson, this sabbatical hadn't come a moment too soon. He needed a break from everything related to *Calvin and Hobbes*. He and his wife had moved to Santa Fe, New Mexico, in late 1990, where they had an unlisted telephone number and lived under Melissa's maiden name. For the most part, this allowed Watterson to avoid fans and the press. He could relax and recoup. While Melissa became a vibrant member of the local quilters guild, Watterson spent a lot of his new-found spare time pursuing hobbies. Martin Garhart, his art professor at Kenyon, lived in the area and the two would meet up to go mountain biking or to paint. "We had a lot of fun together," Garhart remembers. "It was no longer student and teacher; it was just two guys who liked to do a couple of things really well."

Around this time, Lynn Johnston and her husband were traveling across country in a small plane and they stopped by to see the cartoonist and his wife. Watterson and Johnston had corresponded over the years, though this trip would be the first time they had met.

"They were very cordial and very generous," Johnston remembered. "We really had a wonderful visit with them. He did say at the time that he was off the scale when it came to introverted and that he really was uncomfortable with company. So I felt quite honored that he would allow us to come to his home." After this visit, Watterson gave Johnston one of his Sunday strips that he hand-colored for her. It's still up on Johnston's wall in her studio and she says it never fails to make her smile.

According to people with whom I spoke, Watterson felt rejuvenated by his time in Santa Fe, but he was still unhappy with the constraints newspapers were placing on him as an artist. So, he proposed a new, redesigned format for his Sunday strips that allowed him greater flexibility. He had long complained about the confines of the comics section, even bringing it up in his 11 November 1987 strip. In the four-panel strip, Calvin says to Hobbes, "Grandpa says the comics were a lot better years ago when the newspapers printed them bigger. He says comics now are just a bunch of Xeroxed talking heads because there's no space to tell a decent story or to show any interaction." There's a visual gag here that you're missing: the art for every panel is exactly the same and features Calvin's head talking up at Hobbes's. Despite all his public and private griping, Watterson never seemed confident that anything would change when it came to the size of the comics.

So it must have come as a shock to the cartoonist when Universal offered to sell his Sunday strips as unbreakable half pages. This was "more space than I'd dared to ask for," Watterson later wrote in *Sunday Pages 1985–1995*. Under the old format, Sunday strips were drawn in three rows of equal height with one panel division required within each of those rows. Editors would then reconfigure or shrink these rows to accommodate the needs of their comics section. Oftentimes, they would throw away the entire top row, so they could fit even more Sunday strips on a single page. For someone like Watterson who took his art and his writing so seriously, these limitations were at best a continual aggravation, and at worst a severe curtailing of his artistic vision.

Under the new format, editors had to take *Calvin and Hobbes* on Sunday as a single chunk, though they could choose to shrink it down. There would be no cutting off the top row or rearranging any of the panels. Readers would get to see the strip as Watterson wanted them to see it, or not at all. This new format opened up a new world of possibilities to Watterson. "I could write and draw the strip exactly as I imagined it, so it truly challenged my abilities," he wrote in *Sunday Pages 1985–1995*. Like most things worth having, it came at a cost, and that cost was time and energy. Sundays had always taken him about a day to do, but the new format required a day and a half. "I had to steal that extra time from what would have been some semblance of an ordinary life," Watterson wrote. "But I was thrilled to expand the strip's world."

In 1991, the syndicate sent out to the papers that subscribed to the strip an interview with Watterson. The goal of this was to answer the inevitable questions regarding the new format mandate. "Editors will have to judge for themselves whether or not *Calvin and Hobbes* deserves the extra space," he declared. "If they don't think the strip carries its own weight, they don't have to run it. I'm simply saying that if they want the strip, they can't chop it up and reduce it any more."

Watterson knew that in addition to alienating the papers he was syndicated in, he also risked angering some of his fellow cartoonists, since his layout requirements might force other artists off the page. "Of course, the comics pages have always been extremely competitive, and every cartoonist gets his space by taking it away from another cartoonist," Watterson admitted. "It's a dog-eat-dog business in a lot of ways, but I don't have any problem with the idea that a comic strip should be extraordinary to survive." The interview wasn't bereft of humor. Watterson promised "no other comic strip will have bigger, uglier aliens" and included a brief bio in which he claimed to be an amateur space explorer and backyard paleontologist who "publishes his research in his comic strip."

As was expected, the syndicate got some incensed pushback from the papers. Watterson wrote that syndicate reps were thrown out of editors' offices, and threatened cancellations poured into the Universal offices. The American Association of Sunday and Feature Editors asked Universal to reconsider the Sunday size requirement for *Calvin and Hobbes* strips. The president, Barbara Schuler, wrote in a letter that the new format "appears to be yet one more attempt by Universal to dictate how we edit our sections." Universal refused and, though 12 to 15 papers threatened to pull the strip, in the end only seven did. *Calvin and Hobbes* was still appearing in over 1,800 papers, continuing its dominance as one of the most popular strips in the world.

After nine long, dry months, *Calvin and Hobbes* returned to the funny pages on Sunday, 2 February 1992 in the new half-page format. The first one out of the gate really exemplified what Watterson was able to do with his new-found freedom. There were squares, rectangles and circles, some overlapping, but all coming together to form a compelling story. Understanding that his readers might be confused with the new layout, each of the eight panels is numbered, drawing the readers through as Calvin ponders the age old "journey vs. destination" argument to Hobbes, who's holding on to the back of the sled for dear life.

In the coming weeks, Watterson's Sundays included a variety of panel shapes and sizes, putting some at odd angles and adding borders to others. It was a noticeable difference and no one else on the page — with the lone exception of Berke Breathed — ever came close to competing with him. And since there were no "throwaway" panels at the top of his strip, he could tell more complex and visually interesting stories.

The same year Watterson began his new Sunday format, he also released an anthology, *The Indispensable Calvin and Hobbes.* The book begins with a poem, "That many times a simple choice can prove to be essential / Even though it often might appear inconsequential." Later the narrator bemoans his fate, "For no reason I can think of, I've wandered far astray /And that is how I got to where I find myself today." Though the poem's narrator is ostensibly Calvin, these introspective verses reflected Watterson's own internal debates.

Even though he'd gotten everything he thought he wanted — control and ownership of his strip, as well as a larger format — he was still unhappy. During this year, he spent a lot of time thinking about what he really wanted to do, but couldn't envision a conclusion in which he continued to draw the strip. If he wanted to maintain even a modicum of sanity he was going to have to quit. "1992 was the year we knew it was definitely going to end," Salem told me. Universal wasn't sure when Watterson would draw his last panel, but they knew for sure that it was going to happen.

In the months leading up to his retirement, Watterson remained incredibly prolific. He released *Attack of the Deranged Mutant Killer Monster Snow Goons* and *The Indispensable Calvin and Hobbes* in 1992, with *These Days Are Just Packed* following a year later and *Homicidal Psycho Jungle Cat* the year after that. He even took time to do the artwork for his brother Tom's band, the Rels. One cassette sleeve is a woodcut of a man with electrodes attached to his skull and the other is an oil painting of a couple dancing. Both pieces are credited to a Fang Wampire. I have no idea what this means, just like people who didn't know my friends growing up wouldn't have known what nicknames like B-Boi, Sully and Poetry in Motion meant out of context.

But after this flurry of activity and a return to normalcy on the comics page, Watterson dropped another H-Bomb on his readers in 1994: he was going to take *another* nine-month sabbatical. "Bill wants to get away from the daily grind for a while and do a lot of painting, like he did during his first break," Lee Salem told *Editor & Publisher* at the time. "He wants to regenerate himself." Pre-empting the inevitable outcry, Salem attempted to defend his cartoonist. "It's difficult for those who are not creative to judge the pressures faced by those who are. Some cartoonists can work for years without a break while others need one. We have to be flexible . . . He puts himself entirely into the strip. The toll is considerable."

"Taking [two sabbaticals] within three years of each other, I became the Lazy Cartoonist poster boy," Watterson later admitted in *The Calvin and Hobbes Tenth Anniversary Book*. "Some other cartoonists have publicly denounced these vacations as unnecessary and self-indulgent," he continued. "Some cartoonists can meet their own standards of quality and be on the golf course by noon, but that's not the case for everyone. In my opinion, any creative person can be forgiven some occasional time off to recharge the batteries and pursue other interests."

The sabbatical started on 3 April 1994 and ended with the strip's return on 1 January 1995. Watterson came back again on a Sunday with an eye-catching strip featuring tyrannosaurs in F-14s that quickly gained classic status with fans. "This one was a little tricky," Watterson admitted in *Sunday Pages 1985–1995*. "*T. rex* anatomy doesn't fit easily into an airplane cockpit, and it required a little fudging."

This brilliant strip was the bright flash before the explosion. The next 12 months marked *Calvin and Hobbes*'s final run, though only Salem and a few bigwigs at Universal and Andrews and McMeel Publishing knew this. It was a hard time for both parties and everyone was understandably disgruntled for their own reasons. "Our hope was that the readers wouldn't get all the undertones, but obviously some readers did," Salem told me. The 19 October 1995 daily is particularly prescient. "If good things lasted forever, would we appreciate how precious they are?" Hobbes asks Calvin. Shortly after that strip ran, Watterson wrote a letter to his readers that was published in the papers that carried his strip.

> I will be stopping *Calvin and Hobbes* at the end of the year. This was not a recent or an easy decision, and I leave with some sadness. My interests have shifted however, and I believe I've done what I can do within the constraints of daily deadlines and small panels. I am eager to work at a more thoughtful pace, with fewer artistic compromises. I have not yet decided on future projects, but my relationship with Universal Press Syndicate will continue.

That so many newspapers would carry *Calvin and Hobbes* is an honor I'll long be proud of, and I've greatly appreciated your support and indulgence over the last decade. Drawing this comic strip has been a privilege and a pleasure, and I thank you for giving me the opportunity.

Sincerely,

Bill Watterson

To this day, I still remember reading Watterson's letter. I was a junior at Vassar College and one of my parents must have sent me a clipping from our local paper, because as a cash- and time-strapped college student, I had given up on buying and reading newspapers. While I didn't read *Calvin and Hobbes* on a daily basis anymore, I still bought every new book and reveled in going home for the holidays, when I would ensconce myself in my room and reread my entire collection.

It was heartrending to think that something I loved so much and which had given me so much joy over the years was ending. Since the internet hadn't really taken off by then, I didn't go online to hear about conspiracy theories from fellow fans or to see if Watterson had anything more to offer up on the subject of his departure. These days, the creator of a strip that was ending would probably blog about his or her upcoming final strip — or at least grant some interviews to discuss the ending. Watterson did none of this, which made his departure all the more abrupt and confusing. In the wake of the news, the emotion I remember feeling strongest was sadness.

When Watterson's letter was published in hundreds of papers on 9 November 1995, his colleagues and his contemporaries were just as sad as his fans. Lee Salem told *Editor & Publisher*, "[The end of the strip is] a loss for anyone who enjoys comics. Bill brought something really special and different to the comics page." In the same article, *FoxTrot* creator Bill Amend is quoted: "It's very sad news for me. Like most people, I'm a great fan of the strip. Seeing it in the newspaper was like a daily seminar on how to do a good comic. It inspired me and motivated me to be a better cartoonist."

Salem also talked to the *San Francisco Chronicle*, giving further insight into Watterson's decision to retire the strip: "Bill is both refreshingly different and exasperatingly different, depending on one's perspective," he said. "I'm an editor, not a creative person. I think it's difficult for those of us not (creatively) inclined to judge what toll that takes on a person. With some of these people it's a toll they didn't want to pay anymore."

"We were all saying, "Why would you quit drawing when everybody loves the strip?"" Watterson's childhood friend Dr David Bowe told me. "And he'd say, "I'm having to draw stuff I don't like." Towards the end of it, he was putting it out, but he didn't think it was good enough to put out there. And he didn't want to see his cartoon turn into *Peanuts* or *Garfield* — stale writing with the same old jokes."

Mike Peters, creator of *Mother Goose & Grimm*, told me in an interview that he still selfishly wishes that Watterson never stopped. "A strip as good as *Calvin and Hobbes* forces you to sit at the drawing board longer," he confessed. "It forces you to say, "I'm going to try to be better, because this guy is doing inspiring work." When he stopped, I felt hurt by it, because I wanted to have him on the same page, so I could be a lot better."

"When you come up with something that strikes a tone, hits a bell and becomes part of the fabric of people's everyday life, it's almost a responsibility to try to continue that as a long as possible," Peters continued. "Not for any reason other than, God are you lucky. I always think of Humphrey Bogart in *The African Queen*. He says to Katharine Hepburn, "I gotta pull the boat. I gotta get back in with the leeches." It's not what you enjoy, but you're doing a great service. I'm still mad at Watterson; I still want him to come back."

Even Mort Walker, whom Watterson had taken some shots at, was saddened and indignant. "It's too bad when you lose a talent like Watterson, who could add to the breadth of comic strip art and entertain so many people," Walker told me. "You have to know you're entertaining people and making them happy, so to take *Calvin and Hobbes* away from them is not a public service."

When Lynn Johnston heard that Watterson was ending the strip, she shared in the collective sadness, but as a fellow artist and a friend, she empathized with him. She wrote him a letter to express her solidarity. "A lot of people were pressuring him to continue — and that's a wonderful compliment — but at the same time you have your reasons and you have to stick to them," she told me. "I wanted to tell him that I was supporting him." Watterson wrote her back with his thanks, explaining that his retirement was something he needed to do for himself.

It was the last time she would ever hear from Watterson. She wasn't the only one he excommunicated from his life after that either. "People who had been in touch with him, had really supported him, enjoyed his work and loved his creativity, we were quite hurt that he would isolate us," Johnston admitted. "Jim Borgman and I were genuinely friends with him; we really felt that we were all in the same bracket. There are not that many cartoonists; it's a small, emotional community that's very supportive and very caring. So we were surprised that we were no longer on his mailing list. On the other hand, he was always very honest about saying he was very private and we respect that. If I was to run into him again, I would be as warm and as effusive as I always was. I wouldn't feel slighted; I would just say, "That's Bill.""

She also offered her own theory about what may have driven Watterson to finally call it a day. "I think one of the things that pushed him was the fact that his cat Sprite died and he adored this cat. It was one of those big, affectionate cats that are just part of your daily routine. Some cats are private and don't interact with you much, but this one was quite a wonderful pet." Sprite's death inspired a touching Sunday strip in which Calvin and Hobbes grow momentarily sad over the thought that they'll be away from each other when they sleep. But then Calvin has an epiphany: "If we're in each other's dreams, we can play together all night!" The final panel shows the pair each smiling contentedly as they snore.

"People say, "Come on, get over it, it's just a cat,"" she continued. "But they aren't just cats. They're part of your family; they're part of your life. So I think that was just really upsetting for him at a time when he was upset anyways, because he was being pressured to license the strip, to be more visible and to interact with people more." Though this is purely conjecture on Johnston's part, the death of Watterson's cat Sprite, who was a great inspiration for Hobbes, could very well have placed an untenable emotional toll on Watterson at a time when he was already stressed out to the max because of his battles with the syndicate.

Six years later, Watterson gave a more perfunctory explanation of his decision in the introductory essay to *Calvin and Hobbes:*

Sunday Pages 1985–1995: "I wanted to restore some balance to my life. I had given the strip all my time and energy for a decade (and was happy to do so), but now I was that much older and I wanted to work at a more thoughtful pace, out of the limelight, and without the pressures and restrictions of newspapers." Whatever the reason, *Calvin and Hobbes* was over.

The last strip was a half-page Sunday and ran on the last day of the year, 31 December 1995. Watterson's final pronouncement had a Japanese silkscreen quality to it, depicting Calvin and Hobbes sledding down a sparsely sketched, tree-dappled hill. "A new year . . . a fresh, clean start," Hobbes says to Calvin. "It's like having a big white sheet of paper to draw on." As they zip away down the slope — their proverbial ride into the sunset — Calvin says, "Let's go exploring." It was a fitting end to the strip, which had always encouraged readers to use their imaginations to continue Calvin and Hobbes's adventures beyond the page.

Watterson wrote about the last strip in the introductory essay to *Calvin and Hobbes: Sunday Pages 1985–1995*. "I typically colored panel borders and word balloons, but in [the last] strip, I left everything white. Only the characters and the sled were colored, so the drawing would have a very spare and open look to mirror the ideas in the dialogue." Today that final strip hangs in his parents' home in Chagrin Falls. Their son signed it simply, "To Mom and Dad. Love, Bill."

By the time the strip ended, Watterson had sold 23 million *Calvin and Hobbes* books (that number is now over 30 million) and appeared in over 2,400 papers around the world daily, a number bested only by *Garfield* and *Peanuts*. The total of his legacy would be 3,160 strips, and though he only took up a small rectangle of the paper every day (and a larger one every Sunday), his departure left a big hole in the comics page.

To fill this considerable void, newspapers introduced a number of completely new strips. I sympathize with the characters who had to fill Calvin's sneakers and Hobbes's furry feet, because it can't have been easy to compete with the legacy of *Calvin and Hobbes*. The *Washington Post* chose *Over The Hedge* by Michael Fry and T. Lewis and *One Big Happy* by Rick Detorie, though the paper's editors told their readers "We won't try to pretend that they or anything else could make up for the loss of *Calvin and Hobbes*, but they're the best we could come up with."

It's interesting to think of what might have happened if Watterson hadn't wrestled control back from Universal. If the syndicate had controlled the characters, *Calvin and Hobbes* could have gone on without Watterson but using gag writers and artists to do what Watterson had done himself for ten years. Plenty of strips — including one of the first, Richard F. Outcault's *The Yellow Kid* — continue after their creator leaves and some even continue after their creators have died. Today the funny pages are filled with strips whose creators are long dead, including *The Katzenjammer Kids*, *B.C.* and *The Wizard of Id*.

As long as the heirs of the artist or the syndicate which owns the rights want to keep going, stand-in teams can keep producing new strips indefinitely. This is great for brand management of long-running strips with characters who can make the transition from decade to decade and withstand the whims of the public, but it doesn't necessarily make the comics section of the newspaper the cutting edge of artistry, because old standards fill space where new cartoonists might be given a chance at success.

But that wasn't going to happen with *Calvin and Hobbes*. This was it — no one else was going to be allowed to take on the mantle. The strip was over, the daily grind was gone and Watterson could now have the quiet life he and his wife had been looking forward to for several years. They moved back to their hometown of Chagrin Falls in January 1996 and bought an unassuming house on East Washington Street. Local newspaper columnist Barbara Christian wrote a brief article on the couple's arrival, noting "Bill will probably get real irritated with me for reporting this, because he doesn't play the fame game." She went on to appeal to her readers: "[D]o us a favor. Don't ring his doorbell at all times of the day or night, don't stand on the tree lawn and gawk, don't arrive on his doorstep for autographs and don't pose in front of the house holding up C and H books and pointing."

Watterson did get in touch with some old friends following his departure from the comics page, including David Bowe. The pair would meet for breakfast every Tuesday at the local diner, Dink's Restaurant, and hang out for an hour over coffee. A few months after his retirement, *FoxTrot* cartoonist Bill Amend had a chance to see Watterson and his wife. Amend was doing a book signing near Chagrin Falls, so they all had lunch together beforehand. The Wattersons even walked him to the bookstore, where a line was forming. They said their goodbyes and Amend sat down to autograph his books. "I'm not exaggerating when I say every other person in line that day asked me about Bill Watterson," Amend told me in an email exchange. "It was all I could do to not say, "Well, if you go outside, turn right, and walk really fast ...'""

As Watterson was settling back into his old haunts and discovering new pursuits, his cartooning work remained in boxes. By all accounts, he didn't look back at *Calvin and Hobbes*, though he did autograph copies of his collections for the local bookstore, Fireside Books. Besides that, he kept a low profile. In comparison to the one-hit wonders who still tour the state fair circuit, desperately seeking applause for their one moment in the sun, this self-obscuration was highly unusual — though not entirely surprising in Watterson's case. He had never been comfortable with the idea of being a celebrity when his work was popular, so why would he suddenly want to be one now?

Enigma and mystery are in short supply in the era of Web 2.0, 24-hour cable news networks and ever-present cell technology. So, when it exists, people are drawn to it. The entire persona of British graffiti artist Banksy is based on being unidentified and J. D. Salinger still draws more than a few curious souls to his compound in New Hampshire every year. It is because privacy and anonymity are almost impossible to maintain that we appreciate its achievement, even as we paradoxically yearn to get over the proverbial moat and into the fortress.

Watterson's reticence to interact with the public after *Calvin and Hobbes* has drawn some professional curiosity seekers and there have been several fruitless journalistic expeditions to hunt down the cartoonist. The *Plain Dealer* sent a reporter in 1998 and in late 2003; the *Cleveland Scene*'s James Renner traveled to Chagrin Falls; the *Washington Post*'s Gene Weingarten flew in unannounced in 2003, hoping for the scoop of a lifetime. All three journalists came home empty-handed.

"He would like it all to fade away," Watterson's father told the *Plain Dealer* in 1998. "He doesn't get his kicks by being famous. He was just doing something he enjoyed doing." His mother added in the same article, "He definitely wants to disappear. What he likes is that he's two years from the time he did anything, and people are beginning to forget it." Though the general public may have forgotten him, the mystery of Bill Watterson started to become the heated topic of conversation in online forums, late night Comic-Con drinking sessions and at cartoonist conferences. No one knew what he was doing, so everyone tried to out-conjecture each other.

Everyone I spoke to for this book had a Watterson story. Most of them were based on something they had heard from a friend of a friend — they couldn't remember who or when. One story that has been confirmed by both Lee Salem and Rich West is that Watterson has been devoting himself to painting oil-on-canvas landscapes (he included an example of one in *The Complete Calvin and Hobbes*). However, there's an attached rumor that Watterson was burning his first 500 paintings, because he felt they wouldn't be masterful enough. I asked West if he's heard this rumor. "I haven't heard that apocryphal story," West admitted with an air of bemusement. "But it's not far from the truth; he's destroyed many more paintings than he's saved. So I don't know if he's following that method, but he's certainly merciless."

In the introductory essay to the *Sunday Pages*, Watterson wrote, "I've been teaching myself how to paint, and trying to learn something about music. I have no background in either subject, and there are certainly days when I wonder what made me trade proficiency and understanding in one field for clumsiness and ignorance in these others." In another interview, he claimed to be studying a wide variety of artists who struck his fancy, including the Italian Renaissance painter Titian and the abstract expressionist Willem de Kooning. "I'm not a fine artist who has come to cartooning,"

Watterson admitted to *The Comics Journal*. "I drew cartoons all my life and never learned how to really draw until fairly recently." He admitted that it had made his latest artistic efforts cut two ways. "I find it very exciting because it's all new," Watterson revealed. "But it's also frustrating because I'm not good at it. And, also, I enjoy the completely different approach to art where you don't have to worry about writing at the same time."

"He's still searching for his style," West revealed to me. "He's an extraordinarily accomplished painter and he has the fundamentals of composition, coloring and technique down to a fine art. He's studied and has a very clear idea of what he wants to accomplish on the canvas. The problem is that he is very demanding of himself and his clarity does not extend throughout the creation process. So, he has mastered the technique, but he still isn't happy with the final results. And so that pushes him to continue to try and create." According to West, his paintings can be divided into three categories: landscapes, "whimsical stuff" and self-portraits. Some of his more fantastical efforts and his self-portraits are, supposedly, easily identifiable as Watterson's. "But if the landscape works weren't signed, it would be very difficult for anyone to say, "This is the work of the guy who did *Calvin and Hobbes*,"" West revealed.

During the years immediately following his momentous departure from newspapers, Watterson concentrated on painting and his family. He and his wife adopted a baby daughter, Violet, and he became a devoted father by everyone's estimation. (I wasn't able to divine if Violet was already named by the time of the adoption, but it bears noting that there was a lesser-known character in *Peanuts* with the same name.) Aside from the occasional call with Lee Salem to discuss ongoing business matters, Watterson moved on with his life.

Then, on 10 September 2001, six years after he had called it quits, the Ohio State University Cartoon Research Library (now known as the Cartoon Library & Museum) opened the first exhibition ever of Watterson's *Calvin and Hobbes* work. Curator Lucy Caswell worked with the reticent artist to select 36 original Sunday strips — replete with whited-out mistakes and pencil marks — alongside the final, colored versions that appeared in papers. Watterson wrote commentary to accompany the strips, noting everything from their inspiration to his artistic techniques.

For those not lucky enough to attend the exhibitions (which also had a limited run at San Francisco's Cartoon Art Museum in 2002), Watterson published *Calvin and Hobbes: Sunday Pages 1985–1995*. Its introductory essay opens with a shocking revelation: "It's been five years since the end of *Calvin and Hobbes*, the longest time I can remember in which I haven't drawn cartoons." Here he was, one of the greatest artists of the late twentieth century, unrepentantly admitting he had given up practicing the art that made him so famous and helped him earn himself a place in history. Pretty stunning stuff, but stated so matter-of-factly that you get the sense that he knows he made the right decision.

Though Watterson abstained from public participation, his work alone was enough to bring in massive throngs of people. Andrew Farago, the current gallery manager and curator at the Cartoon Art Museum told me that it was by far their most popular exhibit of all time. And Caswell told me that so many people flocked to the tiny reading room of the Cartoon Research Library where the exhibit was hung that oftentimes there was a line of people waiting to get in.

If anything, the exhibit did get Watterson thinking about his legacy and the hundreds of *Calvin and Hobbes* strips and related materials he had in storage. He had been loath to touch them for years, but he knew that he couldn't just let the stuff rot in his attic. "Anybody who is making decisions about life work has to do it on their own time," Caswell pointed out. "We want to assist and support decisions, but it's never on our time; it's on their time. Bill was aware of the fact that we were very interested in having his work here and we left the option open. He was pleased with how the show and the book looked, so after that he was ready to make some choices."

Four years after the show and with no public fanfare, Watterson quietly deposited the entirety of his *Calvin and Hobbes* collection with the Cartoon Research Library on 11 February 2005. He included rare artwork for the collections and calendars, as well as some promotional materials Universal created for the strip. Sadly, he also deposited most — if not all — of the work other cartoonists had given him, including original, inscribed strips from Lynn Johnston, Jim Borgman and Bill Amend. It seems that he didn't want to leave any memories of his cartooning years lying around.

For OSU, this was a huge coup. "It's a remarkable collection, because it is so intact," Caswell told me. "I don't think we know any other major cartoonist who retained as much of his work." Associate Curator Jenny Robb added, "I have heard of artists who have destroyed all — or at least some large portion of their originals — of their cartoons. That makes me sick. I'm thrilled that Bill Watterson decided to put his work on deposit here instead of taking that route." Considering the lengths he has gone to privatize his history, I don't think I would have been surprised if Watterson had done that, but I would have been inestimably saddened.

In 2005, Watterson placed the final nail in the coffin of his creation by putting out *The Complete Calvin and Hobbes*. The massive, three-tome collection weighed 23 pounds and included all 3,160 *Calvin and Hobbes* strips. Watterson also included all the incidental art from his previous collections, several new sketches of his characters for the covers and the slipcase, as well as a lengthy essay.

Designer Michael Reagan, who had overseen Gary Larson's *The Complete Far Side 1980–1994*, was called in to work on the project. Though it took some convincing by Reagan and Tom Thornton from Andrews and McMeel to get Watterson to agree, the project moved forward in the winter of 2003. Reagan would spend the next year and a half on the project, and though it was a difficult, time-consuming process, it was one he still talks about with undiminished joy. "My favorite moment was the first time I got some cover ideas from Bill," Reagan revealed. "He hadn't drawn anything in ten years, but one day you open this package and it's this incredible new work. That was amazing."

One idea that Reagan had for the collection was to enclose the three volumes in a slipcase that looked like the cardboard boxes Calvin used to make transmogrifiers and time machines. "Watterson didn't want to do that," Reagan confided. "He thought that was too tricky. He was intrigued by it, but in the end he just wanted something straightforward. And that worked."

The collection was an obsessive-compulsive collector's dream and a pretty kick-ass Christmas gift for anyone with a sense of humor. Pulitzer Prize-winning comic artist Art Spiegelman, reviewing the collection in *Publishers Weekly*, wrote, "These books offer a testament to Watterson's dedication and to the medium's ability to keep reinventing itself against all odds." The $150 collection became the heaviest book — and one of the most expensive — to ever hit the *New York Times* best-seller list, clocking in at number 4. The *Times* itself noted, "It is so big and dense and beautifully printed and huge that I have real difficulty carrying it from one room to the next. It is worth the work, and worth every penny."

For the release of the collection, fans submitted questions online to Watterson's publisher. Surprisingly, the noted recluse gamely answered a number of them, before a fan asked him what books he read over and over, at which point Watterson ended the Q&A session abruptly, saying, "Hmm. Suddenly I feel very shallow." He popped up two years later, on 12 October 2007, when he surprised unsuspecting *Wall Street Journal* readers by writing a largely positive review of David Michaelis's controversial Schulz biography. Even this short piece provoked a monsoon of internet discussions, leading people to wonder if he might be gearing up for a return. He wasn't.

Watterson vanished back into the woodwork, another guy you could pass on the street without looking twice. He remains wreathed in enigma and mystery, one man standing alone out of the spotlight, though he sometimes finds himself looking back. "Occasionally he'll stumble onto a website where they're having intense discussions about *Calvin and Hobbes*," West revealed. "And they're talking about what an asshole he was for doing X or Y or refusing to make the toys. Bill says he just turns off the computer when he's done and he just blinks and thinks, "What the hell is that? The story is done. Give it up. Get a life.""

That's easy for him to say; everyone else is waiting to see what he does next.

CHAPTER 8

Under the Influence

Watterson sets the bar for art, whimsy and fabulous animated imagery. You could just feel the movement, the excitement and the noise in *Calvin and Hobbes*. Every animator desperately wanted to get their hands on those characters because they could feel the energy inside it. That's what the readers felt. If you can feel the action in something, it just goes right into your breastbone and vibrates. It's as exciting as anything can be.

— Lynn Johnston, creator of *For Better or For Worse*

When I began this project, I'll admit that there were some parts of it I was more excited about than others. One aspect I was really looking forward to was talking to all the cartoonists that Watterson had influenced. The child in me was eager to be paid to chat about the comics, while my coldly professional journalist side wanted to get a factually accurate account of the impression Watterson made on the art of cartooning from those that had experienced it first hand. I started by compiling a list of longtime cartoonists whose work I knew. This was easy; I just went into my childhood bedroom and combed the bookshelves, making notes and stopping occasionally to read when this research became too grueling or I felt "compelled" to have a good laugh.

My work became harder when I started trying to amass a catalog of cartoonists whose work debuted after my newspaper subscription lapsed in the early '90s. I needed a jump-start, so, as with many research projects undertaken in the last few years, I began with Google. I typed in something along the lines of "Bill Watterson + influence + cartoonist" and scrolled through the results. A name that came up a few times was that of Richard Thompson, the artist behind *Cul de Sac*. Apparently, Thompson maintained a blog, where I spent the next hour of my life chuckling.

I was instantly a fan. Thompson's quirky family strip *Cul de Sac* looks like Ralph Steadman and Charles Schulz fighting over a pen to draw *The Yellow Kid* crossed with *FoxTrot*, with a dollop of Watterson's wit thrown in for good measure. His other comic, the weekly *Richard Poor's Almanac*, deals with anything and everything from weather and the Oscars to politics and Valentine's Day. The humor is charmingly unorthodox and the angle is always unexpected; it was a pleasure to discover and I hoped I would be able to meet him.

As luck would have it, Thompson lived across the Potomac River in Arlington, Virginia. After an amusing email exchange, he agreed to meet me for an interview at a hipster java joint called Murky Coffee a few weeks later. I was very excited that I was actually going to have face-to-face dialogue with a cartoonist. I have interviewed all sorts of rock stars over the years, but this was my entrée into a completely different circle with another set of rules and norms. A cartoonist's stage is their workshop, attic or basement, and they aren't ever around when their audience guffawed, applauded or failed to get the joke. I assumed that even the biggest names wouldn't act like Gene Simmons (actually, let's hope that no one acts like that), but I wasn't sure what this breed of artist would be like. Would they be shy and retiring? Would they be like stand-up comedians armed with brushes and pens? Or maybe they would be average Joes and Janes who were just working to make a living. I really had no idea.

Since the coffee shop was jam-packed with Brooklyn refugees in thrift-shop garb typing vigorously on their Mac laptops, we sat outside in the chilly air watching the foot traffic. I sipped something called the Five Dollar Hot Chocolate (which comes with this instructional warning: "12 ounces, FIVE dollars, no modifications, NO QUESTIONS ASKED"), while Thompson had coffee. What Thompson quickly taught me was that cartoonists like to talk. No, they **LOVE** to talk. This is not making a generalization or assigning a stereotype, this is the God's honest truth. I didn't interview a single cartoonist who didn't chat for longer than they had originally allotted.

Thompson set the bar when what was supposed to be a half-hour chat turned into an hour-and-a-half-long conversation. "*Calvin and Hobbes* is still the benchmark of the last thirty years when it comes to instantly classic strips," Thompson told me, as his breath made little clouds that mingled with the steam rising from his coffee. "It's hard to touch upon the subjects he did without infringing on the territory." From there we went on to talk about the presidential race, killer snowmen and why Schulz was a genius until it got cold and dark enough out for us to realize that we should probably get home to our respective lives.

Though Thompson admitted to me that he knew Watterson

informally through a mutual friend, he begged off any real knowledge of his whereabouts or doings. So, I was a little surprised a few weeks later when I discovered that Watterson had decided to come out of hiding to write the foreword to Thompson's forthcoming *Cul de Sac* collection, *This Exit.* "I thought the best newspaper comic strips were long gone, and I've never been happier to be wrong," Watterson wrote. "Richard Thompson's *Cul de Sac* has it all — intelligence, gentle humor, a delightful way with words, and, most surprising of all, wonderful, wonderful drawings."

Later in the same piece, he continues his praise for Thompson's artwork. "With a mix of rambling looseness, blotchy crudeness, and sheer cartoony grace, Thompson's expressive pen line is the equal of any of cartooning's Old Masters. Thompson has a very sharp eye and a command of technique we almost never see anymore. He reminds us that comics can be more than illustrated gag writing, and that good drawings can bring a comic strip's world to life in countless ways that words cannot. The artwork in *Cul de Sac* bowls me over. It's a pleasure to study long after the strips are read."

"It'll likely leave readers disappointed when they reach the actual non-*Calvin and Hobbes* contents, but by then it'll be too late," Thompson quipped to me in an email a few weeks afterwards, before admitting that he was flattered that Watterson had agreed to write the introduction. I was a little disappointed that I had only gotten close to my subject by proxy. He had once again slipped through my fingers. Damn it, I was so close!

To keep my frustration in check, I moved down my hit list to Stephan Pastis, the snarky wunderkind behind *Pearls Before Swine* and a recommendation of Thompson's. Pastis is one of those guys who always gets props from his peers and, after you read a few of his strips or spend some time on the phone with him, you quickly understand why. I liked him because he swore more and made more music references than all my other subjects combined, which made me feel like I was talking to Paul Westerberg or Robert Plant rather than a cartoonist. Making Dylan references while dropping cuss words casually was familiar ground to me, unlike parsing Schulz's declining line work or the merits of *Krazy Kat*.

I knew the interview was going to go well when Pastis began by declaring, "The comics page is mostly utter shit. It sucks." As I was laughing, he was tumbling on. "I know that and so does everybody else, except maybe people in their eighties. It's like entertaining the Shriner's Hall — it's all old, stupid comedy." I love a truth teller and Pastis had no problem letting it all out. "I'm pretty sure that Watterson would totally hate my strip," he declared later in our conversation. "He's very art based and I'm pretty sure he deplores the *Dilbert/Pearls Before Swine* minimal art thing. But that doesn't stop me from admiring him, because I know my weaknesses."

It also doesn't prevent him from borrowing from Watterson wholeheartedly and unabashedly. "I go back to Calvin for facial expressions," Pastis admitted. "There's a Sunday strip where he's either chewing something — or he doesn't like the taste of it — and there are at least 20 expressions. I think Watterson even invented some new ones."

Whenever I interviewed a cartoonist, I would always ask them whom they thought I should be talking with and they would invariably reel off a list of names. Some I'd recognize and others sent me back to Google. Pastis recommended I speak with Bill Amend, the creator of *FoxTrot* and a close friend of his. Though I wasn't a huge fan of the strip, I vaguely remembered that it involved an iguana and a teenager who liked rock 'n' roll, but other than that, the details were hazier than my freshman year of college. I reread some of his works at the library so I knew what I was talking about (I highly recommend *Camp FoxTrot*), then reached out in an email for an interview, which he graciously squeezed into his busy schedule.

It turns out that Amend made Watterson's acquaintance more than 20 years ago, after he sent Watterson a Christmas card. This unsolicited kindness spawned a correspondence friendship and a long-lasting respect between the two artists. "*Calvin* was the one strip running in papers that always made me feel inadequate as a cartoonist," Amend admitted during an email exchange. "It always made me want to raise my game and after it left papers, I really missed that. Bill's thoughts about approaching cartooning as art first and foremost were also inspirational."

Early on, Amend asked if Watterson would be kind enough to write a foreword to his forthcoming *FoxTrot* collection and Watterson agreed. "It's refreshing to read a comic strip where the characters have real personality," Watterson wrote in his essay. "The humor and appeal of *FoxTrot* derive from the interaction of its characters, not from silly events imposed from without. Each member of the Fox family has a unique identity that goes beyond his or her role in the household, and this gives the world of *FoxTrot* a veracity other family strips lack. The Fox family has the resonance of honest observation." He ends by writing, "Surprise is the base of all humor, and nothing is more surprising than the truth. *FoxTrot* has the ring of truth to it."

Amend was the first of many cartoonists who spoke with me about Watterson's inspirational artistry. He recounted a story Watterson told him about trying to get the right look for a giant fly in the strip. Rather than use a traditional brush or pen, Watterson ended up using a stick from his backyard to capture the spirit of the micro-monster he was sketching. "When you consider how rushed and on deadline we cartoonists tend to work, that sort of extra outside-the-box effort is remarkable," Amend admitted. "Not to mention that in this high-tech age, it's refreshing to see such a low-tech approach."

"*Calvin and Hobbes* is the whole package," cartoonist Jeff Smith told me over the phone from his place in Ohio. "You've got really good writing and really good artwork." I was familiar with Smith's *Bone* and thought it was one of the best graphic novels of the last 20 years. Getting him on the phone was a pleasure and a privilege. Getting him to talk about Watterson was just plain fun. "From the very beginning, Bill Watterson was making decisions on how to pace the story and what moment to draw that were pretty unique at the time," revealed Smith. "When you're choosing that moment to pick, what do you draw? Bill often picked off-kilter moments. In one panel, Hobbes would be standing and in the next one Hobbes's head is buried under a couch. Watterson would shoot further than most people would and expect the reader to be with him the whole time."

Smith actually met Watterson a couple of times in the late '80s at Ohio State University for various Cartoon Research Library events. They corresponded, and Smith even sent Watterson some of his work, which he remembers Watterson commenting on favorably. Despite having gone on to considerable comic fame himself, Smith is still reverent. "Bill was one of those humorists like Walt Kelly and Mark Twain," he theorized. "Before you get to the point, they take you on a little journey that drops the point on you in an expected way. They know what they want to say, but they hand it to you in a new way so that it's illuminated and you're surprised by it."

Nicholas Gurewitch, who created the now-retired surrealist romp *The Perry Bible Fellowship*, is a fellow Syracuse University alum. He had gotten his start at the school paper, *The Daily Orange*, and his strip still ran there when I attended years later while earning my graduate degree. I always enjoyed reading his cartoon because of its clever juxtaposition of the whimsical and the macabre. Though his work isn't an obvious offshoot of Watterson's, it was clear from our conversation that the *Calvin and Hobbes* creator had a special place in his heart. "Watterson influenced me big time," he admitted without pretense. "I was simply humbled by him; the way he draws dinosaurs and trees should humble anyone. Though I shied away from his style of doing things, I ultimately aspired to capture things the way he does. Though the humor in my strip is more of a homage to *The Far Side*, *Calvin and Hobbes* laid down everything I needed to know so I could brandish my own style of humor."

Jan Eliot, the mastermind behind *Stone Soup*, was not someone whose work I knew prior to writing this book, but it was a pleasure spending half an hour online with her creation in the name of research. Though her strip deals with a single working mother dealing with more drama than an episode of *Bridezillas*, I enjoyed getting a peek into another perspective and another world. I caught up with her by phone early one morning, and she shared her list of three reasons why Bill Watterson is her hero. "The first reason is that I don't think there has been a more original cartoonist, ever," Eliot declared. "Some days it's intimidating to think of what you could do in a cartoon that Watterson hasn't already done and done so well. Secondly, I learned so much about drawing cartoons from him, especially body movement and facial expression." Even now, she keeps a *Calvin and Hobbes* collection next to her drawing table for when she needs inspiration.

"But my third reason that he's my hero is that he retired the quarter I was launched," she continued with a chuckle. "And so — by no intention of his own — I benefited from the fact that there were hundreds of new spaces open. And because of him retiring cleanly and not doing reruns, I had a terrific launch and was able to make a living within six months of starting my comic strip, which is not necessarily the case of a lot of people."

After Eliot I had the pleasure of speaking with Mark Parisi, who does the topical one-panel strip *Off The Mark*. Watterson's work affected Parisi's own style in a fundamental way. "He made me think about the drawing," he revealed over the phone. "I was going back and forth between having deadpan expressions and very over-the-top expressions, and he made it okay to go for the over-the-top. Watterson brought back that exaggeration without making it plastic."

Parisi also had a personal connection to Watterson. When Parisi was first starting out, he sent Watterson some early *Off The Mark* strips for feedback. Much to his surprise he got a response. "It said something to the effect that he thought some of my ideas were a little too violent, but I should send them to a syndicate," Parisi remembers. "My original reaction was, "Oh, he's not telling me how wonderful I am?" Because that's all cartoonists really want when they send their stuff out. It took me a couple of years before I realized that he was right and that I couldn't really get away with some of the things I wanted to draw. He made me realize that you have to be creative and only suggest violence as opposed to drawing it."

Parisi, never shy about his love of Watterson, has drawn four cartoons featuring Calvin and/or Hobbes. The most famous ran two days after *Calvin and Hobbes* ended. It featured a bloated Hobbes doll burping while Calvin's parents look askance in the living room. The caption reads, "What really happened to Calvin." "I try to work in what is popular at the time and *Calvin and Hobbes* was one of those strips that permeated everyone's consciousness," Parisi explained. "When Watterson retired, that became an opportunity for me to comment." Parisi still doesn't know whether Watterson read any of his *Calvin and Hobbes* homages, though he got a lot of positive feedback from readers.

Mark Tatulli, the creator of *Lio* and *Heart of the City*, didn't fare so well with his readers when he drew a Sunday *Lio* that featured a dead Calvin and Hobbes — it drew more hate mail than anything else he had done up to that point in his career. Which is totally understandable, though not necessarily worthy of an angry letter to your local editor. Any time you kill beloved figures — Santa Claus, the Easter Bunny, Mr Rogers, whoever — you're bound to spark up a few fires.

Tatulli didn't mean any disrespect toward his hero and he happily admits to being indebted to Watterson. "I always drew with pens until I saw Calvin and realized Watterson was doing him with a brush," Tatulli told me by phone. "I just loved the energy that the line work had. *Heart of the City* was definitely influenced by *Calvin and Hobbes*."

Some strips didn't even bother with mere influence and decided to simply appropriate Watterson's characters. Steve Troop's *The Adventures of Mayberry Melonpool* (now known simply as *Mayberry Melonpool*) included several *Calvin and Hobbes* characters on a number of occasions. In one *Melonpool*, Calvin, Hobbes and Uncle Max show up, which prompts Troop to include a little disclaimer, "Apologies to Bill Watterson." In a second homage a wistful Mayberry declares, "Sigh . . . I really miss "Calvin and Hobbes."" A third features Mayberry and Austin Powers dancing, a parody of the Sunday in which Calvin and Hobbes groove to classical music cranked up at 78 rpm in the middle of the night.

"When I started out, everybody kept saying, "You're going to be the next Charles Schulz,"" Troop told me wryly, before adding with a chuckle, "I remember thinking to myself, "No, I'd rather be the next Watterson!"" He began *The Adventures of Mayberry Melonpool* a few years after Watterson, Larson and Breathed had left the funny pages and he decided to pay them tribute by including Opus, Calvin and the *The Far Side* kid in a comic limbo. "What I found, though — even though my art style was similar to Watterson's — was that I could not draw Calvin to save my life," Troop told me with a laugh. "The other characters — which I had not followed as closely — I had no problem with though."

I understand this quandary, because I've faced it a few times while writing this book. There have been times when I've typed out a sentence or a paragraph, then sat back and wondered, "What would Bill think about this? Am I getting it all right? Is it balanced or is the inner child in me messing with my objectivity?" Sometimes this self-doubt and nervousness have produced poorer work (that I've hopefully excised with multiple rewrites and careful edits) than I would have if I were writing about something I wasn't passionate about, like *American Idol*, crab cakes or baseball.

Not everyone I spoke with had a problem imitating Watterson's style. Jef Mallett, the cartoonist who draws the lovable and literate

Frazz, hasn't included Calvin or Hobbes in his strip, but he has nevertheless been praised and accused by fans of borrowing from *Calvin and Hobbes*. A lot of this discussion comes from the fact that the main character, a songwriter/janitor named Edwin "Frazz" Frazier, looks a lot like a thirtysomething version of Calvin, replete with blonde spiky hair. "Honestly, I just wanted messy hair so that it would never go in or out of style," Mallett told me by phone from his Michigan home. "Curly hair looks a little too much like Lyle Lovett."

"I never consciously said, "I'm going to do a strip that will be the next *Calvin and Hobbes*,"" Mallett continued. "I don't know who had that much hubris. But by the same token I didn't say, "I'm going to do a comic strip that looks nothing like *Calvin and Hobbes*." How stupid would you have to be to ignore all that influence? So I just did the comic strip that came out of me." Mallett has not been immune to the debate amongst cartoon fans about Watterson's influence and has alluded to it in the strip several times, including a story line in which Frazz and his friend Caulfield develop a game based on Calvinball.

None of this minor controversy has diluted Mallett's love of Watterson's wonderfully realistic creations. "*Calvin and Hobbes* is genuine," Mallett said to me. "It doesn't seem manufactured; it's very, very lifelike. The way Watterson made his characters move was genius. They're flesh and bone, and they're subject to gravity, wind, balance and all the forces of nature and physics. His characters don't look like inflated Macy's Day parade floats; they're *real* characters."

He ended our conversation by talking about Bill Watterson's indelible mark on the funny pages. "We'd have a lot of the same old stuff, but we wouldn't have some of the best stuff," he declared, before recommending I talk to Dave Coverly. Coverly is another Michigan cartoonist and his quirky one-panel *Speed Bump* makes short work of the idiosyncratic lives we lead. Though he is less influenced by Watterson in his own work than others, Coverly had nothing but praise for Watterson. "If he's not the top guy, he's still on the Mount Olympus of cartooning," Coverly told me unabashedly. "I look at the things he writes and think, "I don't know how you can do any better." I just don't. It's not possible to make the perfect comic strip that everyone in the world will think is the best thing ever — humor is too subjective — but he came as close as possible."

Wow, the "God compliment." That's pretty much as high as you go, unless you're Christopher Hitchens, and it would not be the last comparison to the divine. Somehow I ended up speaking with author and illustrator Sandra Boynton. The playful tone she has perfected in her children's books was evident during our email exchange, especially during her enthusiastic blurb about why she liked Watterson's work, ""Like" is too tame," she wrote emphatically. "Maybe REVERE instead. Revere for Watterson's insight, artistry, inventiveness, irreverence, idealism, pacing, theatricality, articulateness, and humanity. And also his moody impatience. *Calvin and Hobbes* is the Zeus of comic strips."

What is up with these cartoonists and their love of Greek mythology? Don't get me wrong, I read my paperback of *D'Aulaire's Book of Greek Myths* so many times that its pages separated from the spine, making it more like *D'Aulaire's Folder of Greek Myths*, but this kind of hero worship usually only happens between fanboys and Joss Whedon at Comic-Con.

One of my most comically literate — and just plain comic — interviews was with Michael Jantze, a talented and all-around swell fellow who drew *The Norm*, a charming strip that followed the adventures and mishaps of a lovable everyman named — you guessed it — Norm. I had read some online forum discussions between fans who felt that Norm was what Calvin would be like as a grown-up, so Jantze seemed like a good candidate for a discussion of Watterson's influence.

I managed to catch up with him by phone in his studio outside San Francisco early on a sunny August morning. I started our conversation by asking him if he thought Norm was an older version of Calvin. "I don't know if that's the case, because Norm had a completely different childhood," Jantze declared, before admitting a larger debt to Watterson. "*The Norm* was vastly influenced by Bill Watterson's art, though. I loved how he drew hands and trees and outdoors stuff. I basically copped all of that; just stole it outright. I apologize. I'll send him a check, though it wouldn't be a very big check."

Jantze was another cartoonist who wrote to Watterson seeking feedback on his work when he was trying to get syndicated. In 1987, he mailed Watterson, along with Schulz and Lynn Johnston, a series of strips called *Normal u.s.a.*, as well as a letter asking for any advice they might be willing to impart. Much to his surprise, all three cartoonists wrote him back generous and helpful notes. Watterson's critique was blunt, but insightful. "On the chance you were serious about wanting any comments, here are a few, take them for whatever they're worth," Watterson wrote. "I think your animal characters integrate unnaturally into your strip. *Bloom County* gets away with talking animals because the whole strip is weird and unnaturalistic.

It seems to me you're drawing two strips here. The melodrama is a bit maudlin for my tastes and I suggest undercutting it with more humor. You can break hearts with a joke too, don't forget."

Watterson ended on a positive note. "Your work is better than much of what I see, so keep at it." Jantze was blown away by the complexity and thoughtfulness of Watterson's appraisal. Over the next year, he completely redid the strip, removing the animals entirely. He mailed the new version off to Watterson, hoping that his newest effort would evoke a more positive response, but Watterson wasn't completely sold. "The strip has improved quite a bit, but the writing still strikes me as too precious; too much angst and self-analysis," Watterson wrote. "Characters do best when they stop telling us what they're thinking and when they start doing things to reveal what they're thinking. Also I think you're trying too hard to make the characters likeable. They all seem sanitized, and therefore they don't ring true. Readers don't care about the characters' relationships if the characters aren't liked individually."

This sent Jantze scrambling back to the drawing board again. He excised the humans from the strip this time and concentrated on animals, renaming the strip *Roadside Manners*. In 1990, he sent Watterson yet another package of work, which earned him another insightful broadside ". . . I still find the writing a bit forced," Watterson opined. "The characters don't appear to be acting out of any inner necessity. Events seem opposed *on* them, instead of developing through them. Put another way, I think the characters need to stop performing and start living . . . I think these characters need more personality, more reason to exist. Worry about that, and the jokes come by themselves."

This was the last time that Jantze and Watterson would correspond.

Roadside Manners was submitted once and then Jantze killed the idea. After much frustration and a period of writer's block, he happened on the idea for *The Norm* when he started keeping a journal of all the embarrassing and silly things that happened to him on a day-to-day basis. Those moments formed the backbone for his strip, which he admits he never would have arrived at without Watterson's guidance. That mentor-student relationship made a big impression, too, and Jantze happily gives advice to up-and-coming cartoonists when he's approached. "You might not like what I have to say," he said with a laugh. "But I am going to give you my honest critique."

All of these genial conversations with cartoonists who loved and knew Watterson offered such a counterpoint to the artist's public persona, or lack thereof. Though he did write back to some readers who sent him fan mail, this was pretty much the extent of his interaction with them. But it was becoming apparent that Watterson had been a vibrant and participatory member of the cartooning community, despite the fact that he never joined the National Cartoonist Society or went to any of the industry's award galas. He wanted to know his peers on his terms and he was lucky and obstinate enough to be able to do so.

To be honest, at this point I was wondering if any cartoonists would diss Watterson in the slightest. Not that a little hero worship and lavish praise doesn't make for great quotes for a book; it's just interesting to find some opposing views on the subject to get a different perspective, like having Pat Buchanan on MSNBC to play the role of the hapless Republican. Though a number of cartoonists didn't agree with Watterson's hardcore stance on merchandising, it took me a long time to find an artist who took issue with the premise of the strip and even then, it was melded to a ton of outright affection.

Hilary Price, the vibrant humorist who draws *Rhymes With Orange* (perhaps the best name for a comic strip, ever) just so happens to be friends with my cousin, Annie, a factoid I learned one morning over breakfast with my Uncle Peter. I was telling him about this book in between sips of a latte and he mentioned Price, though he was sure he got the name of her strip wrong because, "It just doesn't make any sense."

I was able to catch up with Price a few weeks later by phone and she offered the first thoughtful criticism of the strip's conceit. At the heart of her critique was the miniature battle of the sexes that often played out between Calvin and Susie. "That's all very *Dennis the Menace* to me," Price argued. "There's nothing groundbreaking about boys being playful and girls being responsible. So as a girl who didn't fit that stereotype, it was never inspiring to see that stereotype repeated." Finally, some objective feminism! Being the boy throwing slush balls and water balloons, I had spent precious little of my time trying to see things from Susie Derkins' perspective. This isn't to say that Price wasn't a fan, because she found a lot to love in Watterson's work. "The strips that really moved me were the strips about play, taking your time and enjoying the wonder of small things," she revealed. "It reminded you how great it was to be a kid."

By this time, I had spoken to so many cartoonists that I was seeing word bubbles over my wife when she talked. I was feeling burned out on immersing myself in this insular world of comic strips. I needed to get out of it for a while to kick-start my enthusiasm. So, I decided to try to talk to anyone I thought might have a funny take on *Calvin and Hobbes*. After all, this book was becoming my journey as much as it was a trip through Watterson's life, so I might as well have fun doing it.

In high school, I used to get a huge kick out of reading newspaper columnist Dave Barry, because I appreciated the ease with which he lampooned his family and friends. He always did it with love and affection, but he never seemed to hold back when a good drubbing was due. I still have a couple of his books, including a copy of *Dave Barry's Greatest Hits* that I recently unearthed. Though Barry retired from column writing in 2005, I was able to track him down at the offices he still maintains at the *Miami Herald*. We started out by talking about the pressures of constantly delivering for newspapers, a difficulty he shared with Watterson. "You have a tendency to feel that you're a fraud and that everything you've done till now has been luck," he joked. "Or that you've given everything you have to give and now you're living on fumes, reputation and general fraudulence."

Over the course of our half-hour discussion, I tried not to laugh too much as I sat thinking to myself, "Damn, if only eighth-grade Nevin could have known this was going to happen one day. He would have been pretty impressed!" Since Barry, like Watterson, traded so heavily in family situational humor, I asked him what he thought about Watterson's material from that arena. "The best humor is usually what people recognize as being about part of their own lives, rather than something just truly weird," Barry opined. "Family is something familiar to everyone. You can twist it, because it's supposed to be sentimental, sacred, warm and fuzzy, but it's really not much of the time."

"*Calvin and Hobbes* reconfirmed my sense of humor and made me think, "Cool, I'm on the right track,"" comedian/actor Patton Oswalt told me, when I reached him by phone in his Los Angeles-area home. I had become hooked on the comic's hilarious

Werewolves and Lollipops disc a few weeks earlier. I'd been forcing everyone I knew to listen to it when we were in the car, much to the annoyance of my wife, who would rather have been listening to the Arcade Fire or TV On The Radio — anything except Oswalt's joke about going back in time to kill George Lucas . . . again. It turned out that Oswalt grew up outside Washington, DC, in a little burg named Sterling, Virginia (he has something to say about that, too, on *Werewolves and Lollipops*, but I made a vow to limit the obscenities in this book), and he can still remember reading the first *Calvin and Hobbes* when it debuted in the *Washington Post*. "There was a lot of Calvin in my friends and I, the way we imagined other worlds, so we really identified with it right away," he revealed. He loved the fact that Watterson wanted to elevate his readers. "Watterson's reminded you that imagination was more powerful than despair, which was a gentle rebuke of *Peanuts'* total depression. He wanted to remind you that there's always wonder out there."

Around this time, I had finished reading Jonathan Lethem's *The Fortress of Solitude*, which was shot through with comic-book references. I thought he might be a fan of the strip or, at the very least, he might be someone who was literate enough in the topic that he might want to have a conversation about it. I caught up with him late in the summer after he had returned from a trip to Italy and was settling back into the hometown time zone. Our conversation was wide ranging and spiked with sidebars, and was probably the most intellectual discussion of cartooning I'd ever had.

Lethem's love of comics began with a profound affection for classic strips like *Dick Tracy*, *Beetle Bailey*, *Peanuts* and, ultimately, *Krazy Kat*. He didn't have much faith in modern comics, so, at first, he was hesitant to become a fan of *Calvin and Hobbes*, wondering if it might not be able to live up to its clamorous hype. "My first thought was, "Well, people like *Garfield*,"" he remembered to me. "I had a pre-formatted cynicism that modern newspaper strips were pathetic." It wasn't until he read a *Calvin and Hobbes* collection that he really realized what Watterson had accomplished.

After that first collection, he was hooked. "He did something so totally intimate and so weirdly substantial," Lethem told me. He often reread the strips, finding new aspects to appreciate with each new viewing. "Watterson found a rhythm of gently associated sequences of strips," Lethem theorized. "That becomes very hypnotic, just as it does in Schulz, when you realize each strip is a perfect little thing implying a kind of whole universe. You can read them all out of sequence and receive a great impression, but you could also read them day to day and there was this gentle tidal quality to the motifs, where one would tumble into the next. You didn't need the information from the previous — you wouldn't be missing something — but they would have that very sweet, deepening, gentle quality of deepening one to the next."

This rhythmic quality is most apparent to me in certain recurring set-ups like the sled rides, the long walks in the woods, and the late-night conversations in which Calvin and Hobbes seriously parsed the world and their experience in it. These philosophical discussions were always self-contained, but, taken as a whole, they usher you into a complete, well-thought-out worldview that is as deep as it is insightful.

Despite these thoughtful debates, the strip is tinged with an underlying melancholy. Here is a kid with one imaginary friend and no actual friends, constantly trying to escape his reality. "*Calvin and Hobbes* is strangely lonely," Lethem opined to me. "It has an undertow of solecism and darkness that's really interesting. Calvin has this immensity of freedom that comes from an imaginative life, but he also has the maladjustments, or the inaccuracies, that come from preferring his imaginative life."

Another artist outside of the realm of traditional comic stripping I spoke with was Craig Thompson, the creator of the emotionally raw and brutally autobiographical graphic novel *Blankets*. I had quickly fallen for Thompson's imaginatively woven art and soul-searing storytelling. He blended fantasy sequences into his characters' experiences, giving a nightmarish quality to some of the book's darker turns. It turns out that Watterson influenced Thompson in a big way. "I definitely hold him up as one of the most important American artists of all time," Thompson told me over the phone during a break from drawing his forthcoming graphic novel, *Habibi*. "Those moments in *Blankets* where the edge between psychedelic experience and reality blur — like the cave sequence and the shark fantasies when the bed is a boat — that's Watterson's influence."

"I've always wanted my comics to have a musical quality," he continued. "I've always envied how pop music has this ability to create a strong emotional experience. I always saw that quality in Watterson, too." When pressed, Thompson admitted that the pop song he'd most like his work to echo is the Cure's swooning ballad "A Letter to Elise." "It's such a sad little love letter," Thompson explained. Taken from the UK fivesome's 1992 album, *Wish*, the song is sheer heartbreak as Robert Smith keens, "I thought you were the girl I always dreamed about / But I let the dream go / And the promises broke / And the make-believe ran out . . ." It's a keen reminder of just how strong a pull a song can exert on someone in need of solace.

That same quantum of solace can be found in Watterson's land-scapes. The seasons felt real and Watterson's take on the natural world echoed strongly with my love of the woods and quiet places. It's common ground for Thompson. "There's an organic, Henry David Thoreau quality about *Calvin and Hobbes*," he continued. "You could call it pastoral. I really connected with it, because I grew up in the Midwest and that's the backdrop of the strip. It's not an urban comic strip like *Spiderman*; it's about all those poetic, natural places."

I have always had a special affinity for Watterson's winter sequences. Whether Calvin was crafting deranged mutant killer monster snow goons, going sledding or hurling slush balls at Susie, I always felt like I was peering into a cartoon reflection of our world, like I was in a-ha's "Take on Me" video or gazing down a rabbit hole with Alice by my side.

This portion of the book was written during the winter months outside Washington, DC, so I was constantly reminded of the power of Watterson's drawing. There is no snow on the ground — so I have no plans to build a row of Easter Island-styled snowmen in the front yard — but the trees have that same barren, forlorn look that Watterson always captured so deftly. It's hard to express that natural simplicity, never mind having to do it in the cramped, black-and-white quarters of the funny pages.

I wanted to know what natural world informed these bucolic vignettes. Where had Watterson learned to draw these classic land-scapes? It was one thing to hear about, read about and see Watterson's work and to discuss it with those that knew him best, but I wanted to experience the place where he came from to get a tangible sense of the environment that helped shaped *Calvin and Hobbes*. I wanted to smell it, taste it and get a real sense of it. The only way to do that was to go there. I had to go to Watterson's hometown of Chagrin Falls, Ohio. It would be my pilgrimage to a secular Mecca, a road trip into the heartland to discover the soul of my subject.

CHAPTER 9

There and Back Again

Thanks for sharing *Calvin and Hobbes* with us, Bill. I don't think there's anyone who's drawing cartoons who hasn't been influenced in a positive way by your work. We all owe you one.

— Keith Knight, creator of *The K Kronicles*

I have a nightmare. It starts out as a dream; something normal and pleasant and not scary or paranoia-inducing at all. It's morning time, the sun is shining and I'm enjoying a cup of coffee. My phone rings and I pick up: it is Bill Watterson. Without any preamble, he demands that I do an interview with him right then and there.

This is somewhat akin to another recurring nightmare of mine, in which I'm back in high school on what turns out to be exam day for a class I haven't attended all year. Usually it's something like Japanese, advanced physics or advanced Japanese physics where you can't BS your way to a passing grade. I spend the whole dream staring at the test and freaking out because I know I'm going to fail.

But in my latest nightmare, Watterson is on the phone and I don't have any notes or questions prepared. Nonetheless, I don't want to blow my sole opportunity, so I pull myself together and start the interview. I'm nervous at first, but I've been studying this guy for months now, so I seem to be doing well. I'm asking great questions and he's affably giving me wonderful answers. I have achieved the impossible: Bill Watterson is talking to me! Eternal glory and a seat on Olympus with the gods are mine!

Then, as suddenly as he called, he ends the conversation. I'm staring at the lifeless phone in my hand, still astonished by the whole ordeal, when my gaze travels down to my digital recorder and my heart stops — I didn't record any of this. My scream of frustrated disbelief wakes me up and I can't fall back to sleep, although it's 4:30 in the morning.

No doubt my intro gave you an inkling that this was the kind of psychological agita that plagued me at various points during the writing of this book. Though the moments of exhilaration far outweighed my moments of frustration and anxiety, there were still enough stressful junctures to give me a few white hairs. And though the quest to find Bill Watterson and his work was mostly a figurative journey, I did want to turn my search into a literal journey to the heart of Bill Watterson's work. At the very least, it would be nice to tear myself away from the lonely, co-dependent relationship I'd developed with my writing desk.

So in late November 2008, I bought a plane ticket to Ohio and packed up the tools of my trade — a laptop, pens, notebooks, the digital recorder from my nightmare, a big bag of Swedish Fish and a video camera. Cincinnati was frigid when I flew in and the wind's piercing quality reminded me of the winter it had snowed 124.6 inches when I was at graduate school at Syracuse University in Central New York. After picking up my rental car, I drove 45 minutes northeast in the darkness to Mason, Ohio. My dear friend Tomer and his family had moved to these Midwestern hinterlands a few years earlier and I had yet to see their new home. This trip was the perfect way to knock out two birds with one stone.

As I was making my way to their house from the thruway, I was struck by the way the landscape could change from Wal-Marts to farmland with a single turn. The contrast between the neon signs and the darkened fields was jarring. In a single mile you could see America's iconic imagining of its heartland (the Wyeth version) and the reality of it (the strip-mall version); they didn't seem comfortable side by side. In a way, this double vision was like the juxtaposition of Calvin's perception of the world and his parents' differing perception. Everyone's looking at the same thing, but one's subjective reality shapes what we choose to see.

The next morning, armed with the largest cup of coffee I could find, I made my way north to what is now known as the Cartoon Library & Museum (it was still called the Cartoon Research Library when I was there) at Ohio State University in Columbus. The library opened its doors in 1977 after *Terry and the Pirates* and *Steve Canyon* creator Milton Caniff, an OSU alum, donated his personal collection to get the comic repository off the ground. Over the years, he was a vital proponent of the library and helped them acquire Walt Kelly's and Will Eisner's papers, as well as the National Cartoonist Society's archives. As it stands, it is the largest collection of cartoon art in the world, housing 450,000 original cartoons, 3,000 linear feet of manuscript materials and 2.5 million comic strip clippings and tear sheets. It's also the home of Bill Watterson's archives, which makes it ground zero for me.

I arrived just as the museum was opening. Located in an unassuming corner of the arts complex, its understated presence belies the wealth of material hidden in its temperature-controlled archives. A statue of Garfield sits on a bench in the hallway and old printing plates hang on the wall, contrasting scholarly gravitas with childish joy. Inside the library's reading room, researchers must don Mickey Mouse hands — white gloves — and you can use only pencils to keep notes. Requested materials are wheeled out on black metal carts and everything is handled by the librarian on duty, until they decide you're appropriately respectful. After that, you're left to your own devices.

Though it's only 65 degrees in the library (optimum for document preservation), it's not the temperature that sends a chill up my spine when I look at the first *Calvin and Hobbes* strip. Though it ran for only one day, 18 November 1985, it took Watterson a long time to get to that moment. For me, it was exciting on two levels, because I wasn't just holding a key piece of research; I was holding a cherished piece of my childhood.

The strip is drawn on a small piece of slightly yellowed, heavy drawing paper. It's surprisingly insubstantial, but it hums with an inner life. The paper is dotted with cover-ups and faint pencil lines that once guided Watterson's hand. Each dab of Wite-Out, each rough line, each eraser mark was an insight. Sometimes you could see where a word had been changed at the last minute or a facial expression had been altered after a second thought. It's amazing how many mistakes he made, even in this finished product, though as the years went by, these sorts of marks occur with less frequency.

The second strip is even more eye-opening, because I notice things I've never seen before — the lamp has a Charlie Brown zigzag across it, Calvin's eyes remind me of tiny lower case "o"s and the human noses in profile look like sideways horseshoes. Though

I've read this strip a hundred times, it's amazing what looking at it in person does to my appreciation and my understanding of its miniscule details.

This new-found understanding was just the beginning. For the next few hours, I gorged myself on Watterson's artwork, trying not to exclaim with delight in the stillness of the library with each new discovery. Seeing them as singular pieces of art made me appraise them with a new depth and intensity. Each new piece was a mini-epiphany and I filled half a notebook without effort.

Though I viewed a representational sample of Watterson's ten-year run, I made sure to ask for some strips that were just personal favorites. Some made me laugh out loud, some made me hold the page close to my delighted eyes and some made me pause and think. The ones which affected me the most were a series he did in the middle of March 1987. The nine strips form a single storyline in which Calvin and Hobbes come across an injured baby raccoon that subsequently passes away.

Watterson claimed in *The Calvin and Hobbes Tenth Anniversary Book* that this series was inspired by a dead kitten his wife found one morning. "This story not only revealed new facets of Calvin's personality but it also suggested to me that the strip was broad enough to handle a wide range of subjects, ideas, and emotions," he wrote. "The strip's world suddenly opened up." He spoke about the series further when he was interviewed by the *Los Angeles Times*: "I made it a progression from Calvin and Hobbes's emotional response to death through the grieving process to the philosophical aspects," he explained. "Why did this have to happen? If it can happen to a raccoon that hasn't harmed anyone then we all are vulnerable."

Watterson handled the delicate topic with grace and discussed it with a candor that was easy for kids to understand and adults to empathize with. This series is a testament to Watterson's communicative abilities, because he presented the issue in a manner that was easy for everyone to comprehend without dumbing it down so much that it lost all gravity and pathos. In the 14 March strip, Calvin laments, "I'm crying because out there he's gone, but he's not gone inside me." Though a lot of the strips ended without an upbeat punch line, Watterson did include a few moments of levity. In the 11 March strip, Calvin muses, "I read in a book that raccoons will eat just about anything," before quipping, "Chances are, I'll be happy to donate most of my dinner."

Watterson brought up death again in the 19 September 1993 Sunday strip, when Calvin and Hobbes find a dead bird in the woods. The first panel is a stark black-and-white sketch of the deceased. "Not many Sunday strips begin with a panel like this," Watterson declared in *The Calvin and Hobbes Tenth Anniversary Book*. "Once it's too late, you appreciate what a miracle life is," Calvin ponders in the strip. "You realize that nature is ruthless and our existence is very fragile, temporary, and precious." The piece ends with the friends seated under a tree, watching birds fly by. Though it isn't as poignant as the death of the raccoon, it is a nonetheless delicate moment of philosophy so rare in the comics section.

The first death in a comic strip was that of Mary Gold in *The Gumps*, who passed away on 30 April 1929. Though deaths occurred occasionally on the comics page after that, they never occurred frequently. In *For Better or For Worse*, Farley, the family dog, dies while saving April from drowning. Milton Caniff killed off Raven Sherman in *Terry and the Pirates*, and Lippincott, the gay man with AIDS in *Doonesbury*, passed away on the comics page while listening to the Beach Boys' "Wouldn't It Be Nice." In each of these cases, the artist received a lot of mail from their readers and editors, including many angry letters.

Though we are now used to reading dialogue and having a virtual history of contact between artists and their fans in blogs, online comments sections and forum Q&As, correspondence from pre-internet fans is a rarity. Luckily, the museum has in its collection the letters Watterson received from fans about the raccoon strips — and the emotions in these missives run the gamut. Many readers shared heartrending stories of personal loss and how they could connect with Watterson's simple, yet thoughtful, insights. A few complained that death was a verboten topic on the comics page and more than a few writers commented that you shouldn't handle dying animals, as they very well may be rabid. One concerned reader even included pamphlets on what to do if you find a hurt animal. Perhaps the most touching letter came from a Los Angeles schoolteacher, who worked in one of the city's more dangerous and depressed areas. "Please keep drawing *Calvin and Hobbes*," she pleaded. "I need to be reminded of the wonder of childhood. You are my daily mental health break."

After reading all those letters, which was an emotional odyssey itself, I felt the need to take a break of my own and find some psychological sustenance. The Wexner Center for the Arts, just around the corner from the library, was hosting an exhaustive and colorful exhibition of Andy Warhol's many artistic pursuits. Though Watterson never cited Warhol as a reference point, the pop art genius's name did come up once in my research. Watterson fielded a compliment from the interviewer in a piece he did for *Honk!* magazine. "[I]t's gratifying to hear that from people who care about comic art," he graciously responds. "I never know what to make of it when someone writes to say, "*Calvin and Hobbes* is the best strip in the paper. I like it even more than *Nancy*." Ugh." "That's Andy Warhol's favorite strip," the interviewer replies. "Oh, well, that would figure. Maybe he's the nut writing me," Watterson snaps right back.

The Warhol exhibit is an abundance of eye candy, an audio-visual smorgasbord. My eyes quickly became drunk on color and form as I took in the poptastic portraits of Mick Jagger and checked out the album covers display, from *The Velvet Underground and Nico* to *Sticky Fingers*. I even played with the *Silver Clouds* installation — a room filled with Mylar pillow-shaped balloons that you can bat around. This interactive art was located inside a room with floor-to-ceiling windows that look out on the campus. One can only imagine what the college kids who walk by must have thought about the fully grown man unabashedly spoiling his inner child.

Wandering around, I found quotes from the sound-bite-savvy artist scattered across the walls at peculiar heights and in odd corners. One in particular caught my eye, "Pop art is for everyone," and it made me think of Watterson. Even though Watterson hadn't set out to create something with mass appeal, *Calvin and Hobbes* did ultimately attract an audience that was without age limits or cultural boundaries. It was universally understandable without becoming meaningless or trite. Its attractiveness never detracted from its artistry or depth. In that way, the strip was the ultimate piece of pop art. But if Warhol had created it, I imagine we all would have had Hobbes stuffed animals as kids and Calvin coffee mugs as adults.

It was rather odd to walk through this vibrant, multimedia

exhibit and its lavish gift store (where I couldn't resist purchasing the above quote as a print), because it was an exuberant rejection of Watterson's studied simplicity next door. Warhol embraced fame, was inspired by it and fed on it. On the other hand, Watterson hated fame, shunned it and it ultimately helped destroy his passion for cartooning. He probably wouldn't have lasted five minutes at the Factory before running out the door in horror.

The two artists' personas do overlap in the sense that they both managed to negotiate fame on their own terms and confounded the norm in each instance. No one of Watterson's stature had been able to shield themselves as much from success as he did and Warhol managed to become arguably more famous than even the most famous of his superstar subjects. They both manipulated the construct of fame, but with completely different intentions and results.

When my hour of walkabout through Warholia ended, it was odd to sit back down in the simple quietude of the library. The artwork became even more enchanting to me in its stark presentation. I could concentrate on each strip's details, rather than be overwhelmed by the entirety of his output. I checked out more strips and some of the watercolors that Watterson had put on deposit, including those that had been part of his two authorized calendars. Unlike the typical strip, which is done only in black and white, with the colorists adding in color where the artist indicates, these strips were actually painted by Watterson.

In one of these technicolor paintings, Calvin and Hobbes are walking through woodlands alive with what Hobbes calls "Nature's own fireworks display." Burnt oranges, saffron yellows and rich reds mingle with a hint of green in the leaf canopies above the pair.

Another strip, this one set in winter, has a palette of antithetical colors — deep blues, rich purples, blacks and whites — that perfectly capture the colors of Ohio in November and bring its frigid landscape to life.

The only sounds as I looked at these watercolors were the hum of the ventilation system and the keyboard taps from the librarian seated by the front door. I had an out-of-body moment as this Zen soundtrack hummed around me. I saw myself sitting there with piles of Watterson artwork piled around me. I was a cartoon pirate admiring his plunder. It was a long way from the simple kitchen table where I ate breakfast every morning as a teenager. There I'd read *Calvin and Hobbes*, in between bites of wholewheat toast with lemon curd slathered on it, warm oatmeal with raisins or whatever my mother had lovingly whipped up that day.

I felt engulfed by Watterson's story. Art can tell you so much about an artist, but how much have I in fact learned about the man behind *Calvin and Hobbes*? All his corrections imply a perfectionist and his use of natural, organic colors signals that he loves the outdoors. And the very fact that he put his work on deposit means to me that though he may want to distance himself from his work and his legacy, he still recognizes that it is a part of himself no less important on a personal level than it is in the realm of cartooning.

I thought about this, but it just raised more questions. How was Watterson shaped? What made him the man that created *Calvin and Hobbes*? Where did this overly imaginative six-year-old and his tiger spring? Since the strip is so grounded in the childhood experience, I knew that understanding Watterson's own childhood would be key. Chagrin Falls, Ohio is where he spent the majority of his formative years, so maybe it possessed the key to my questions.

The next morning, I got up at 5 a.m. and roused Tomer. Chagrin Falls was over four hours away and there was a lot to accomplish once we got there. I rode shotgun and filmed video out the window as we headed northward, neither of us sure what to expect. Fueled by Caribou Iced Coffee, Krispy Kreme pumpkin-spice donut holes and the Editors' album *An End Has A Start* at full volume, we whizzed across Ohio's flatness in good spirits. We zipped by barren farmlands and two giant billboards displaying the Ten Commandments. It was a little early for "Thou Shalt Not Make Any Graven Images" and I didn't get much sleep, but I was buzzing. Chagrin Falls is the epicenter of my story and I was excited to experience it in the flesh.

After a couple of hours, snow started to appear as light dust on the roadside. As we got closer to our destination, it got deeper and deeper, like a blanket intent on cloaking everything beneath it. As it turned out, it had snowed 18 inches the night before in Chagrin Falls. We hoped to get there after the plows cleared the road, but we weren't sure if we'd be that lucky.

Before my trip, I'd been reading a lot about Watterson's hometown, but my favorite impression came from the artist's work itself. The back cover of *The Essential Calvin and Hobbes* features a Godzilla-sized Calvin rampaging through the center of downtown Chagrin Falls. He's shaking the Popcorn Shop with his massive hands as his gigantic feet stomp ominously towards the bandstand at the center of the town green. This is how I've always imagined Chagrin Falls will be: a place that seems normal on the outside, but has all sorts of mysterious adventures unfolding just behind the façade.

When we arrived, Chagrin Falls stretched out before us like a scene in a Christmas fairy tale. Everything was drenched in pure white, as if God had forgotten to shake the earth as he would a snow globe. Though the roads were mostly clean, it was still a quiet Saturday morning and not many people were out and about. Many of the houses we passed had a rustic, New England sensibility, like some of the small towns in New Hampshire I traveled to with my parents as a kid.

I started my day at the Chagrin Falls Historical Society, located next door to the fire station on a quiet side street a few blocks away from downtown. Its compact exterior belies the wealth of material crammed into its warm interior. In one corner, old iron trivets and piggy banks made at the foundries that used to fuel the Chagrin Falls economy line fill a whole glass-fronted case, while another shelf overflowed with recently donated antique dolls. Old black-and-white photos dotted the walls and one room had an old wooden spinning wheel gathering dust.

Society members Zo Sykora and Pat Zalba were waiting for us, their small assortment of rare Watterson memorabilia proudly laid out on a table in the center room. In this collection there was a signed copy of *The Calvin and Hobbes Tenth Anniversary Book*, Watterson's senior yearbook and a newspaper clipping of one of Watterson's editorial cartoons from 1979.

There was also a note from Bill's mother, Kathryn. "The family of Bill Watterson requests that, when inquiry is made about him, you do not reveal in what state or town he is living, if you know. Most people are interested and kind and respect his wish for privacy. Unfortunately, there have been a few who, given any clue as to his whereabouts, make it a game to find him . . . and let him know they have found him. This is frightening, as you can imagine. I do appreciate your help." Oh Irony, how I love thee, I thought.

Don't worry, Bill, I won't tell anyone where you live and I won't show up on your doorstep; I promise. There's a not-so-fine line between being an investigative writer and a psychotic stalker. I plan on remaining in the former category, but the story must be told. I needed to get out into Chagrin Falls and experience the small town for myself. Zo had appointed herself our tour guide and we were glad to have her. There's nothing better than having a fixer on the ground to open doors and perform introductions. So, without further ado, we headed back out into the snowy morning, the video camera rolling as Zo kept up a running commentary.

Chagrin Falls is one of those bucolic spots that looks picturesque no matter what the season and on the day I visited the whole snowy scene was impeccably delightful. My gut impression was that Chagrin Falls would be a really wonderful place to raise a family. I thought this not withstanding the fact that I was raised in another quaint town like this and I know the downsides to small town life — the wanton isolation and lack of Michelin-reviewed restaurants or art-house cinemas. We walked into the downtown area, which centers around Triangle Park, a sliver of land with a bandstand built back in 1877. From where I stood when I first took in the lie of the land, I was looking down the center of town from the same perspective that Watterson drew Calvin rampaging through this area. When I squinted hard and used my imagination, I could just make out Calvin looming over the end of town.

Up to our left, on the west side of Franklin Street, was Fireside Book Shop, a warm independent bookstore that was another important pit stop. For a while after he retired, Watterson donated signed copies of *Calvin and Hobbes* books to raise money for charities or to help out the bookstore. His mother delivered the books and he never dropped them off personally. However, this activity ended altogether once Watterson discovered some of these copies had made their way onto eBay.

When I talked to the manager on duty, Phil Barress, he told me that he still gets inquiries from fans seeking the signed copies and it's his job to dash their hopes several times a month. There's still a display of unsigned copies of Watterson's work, which Barress tells me sell well and often prompt questions from tourists. He can't remember the last time he saw Watterson around town, though. It wasn't any time recently.

Further up the street is another important location in the Chagrin Falls of *Calvin and Hobbes* fame, the Popcorn Shop. Built in 1875, the shop used to be a retail showcase for the adjoining flourmill, before it became a snack shop in the 1940s. Decorated like a soda shop cross-dressed with a Boho coffee bar, it's an overloaded mash-up of American icons. It's a picture-perfect piece of Americana itself and it's easy to see why Watterson chose it to be such a prominent part of his watercolor of Calvin's devastating frenzy. This impossible-to-miss red, white and blue landmark is perched right above the town's cascading namesake.

Outside the shop, we took a long look at the falls. According to one now-discounted theory, the town's name came from a bastardization of an Indian word for "clear water," though in all likelihood it was named for a French trader, François Saguin. He ran a trading post at the intersection of the Cuyahoga River and Tinkers Creek in the 1740s and earned enough respect from his peers that he was worthy of a small waterfall to be named after him.

Saguin's riverbanks were doused in snow and our breath floated in the air, as the green Chagrin Falls River gushed over the flat rock plateaus with focused energy. Settlers were drawn to these waterfalls in the mid-1700s and they harnessed them to power a number of mills, foundries and factories, which fueled the area's fledgling economy. Though a few mills remain standing today, none of them operate in their original capacity. Now the mills and the falls are mere props in a picturesque photo op, a reminder of a time long passed.

From the falls, we ambled through the center of town, popping into shops and gazing in the windows bedecked with holiday decorations. As I walked, I kept wondering if I'd see Watterson, even though I knew he hadn't lived there for several years. I had these odd visions of him spying on me from behind bushes as I made my way through town. When we entered stores, I felt somewhat bad about asking those inside whether they knew Watterson, because previous reporters have noted that the locals were protective of their home-grown celebrity. However, Watterson is not the only household name associated with Chagrin Falls. Over the years, the small town has been called home by actor Tim Conway (who made his mark in *McHale's Navy*), *Showgirls* scribe Joe Eszterhas and a young Scott Weiland, who would go on to front Stone Temple Pilots.

Despite my anxiety, no one got upset or offended when I asked about Watterson, but no one had any particular insight either. After a few fruitless forays, I gave up on this approach and headed over to the Chagrin Falls High School to meet the director of its alumni association, Tom Mattern. A jovial and approachable guy with a real allegiance to his alma mater, Mattern and his cohorts had set up what they called the Historical Room in a wing of the high school. It's a miniature museum filled with a wealth of material, from yearbooks and awards to newspapers, sports-team archives and photographs.

They even have a few precious Watterson-related items, which Mattern has highlighted in a small display. Alongside an old editorial cartoon and a cartoon he did to immortalize his graduation are a pair of pictures of a young Watterson. One photograph is from a long ago homecoming night and features Watterson and his future wife, Melissa, uncomfortably posed with a larger group. The other is more candid, catching a mustachioed Watterson as he swoops in to give a giggling Melissa a kiss. The pictures are a sweet peek into Bill's high school years and another piece of the puzzle that is Bill Watterson.

By this time, early afternoon had arrived and my list of must-see places was not exhausted. I had yet to see Watterson's childhood home, and though I didn't want to go up and knock on the door, I did want to get a glimpse of it. I had sent a letter to his parents a couple of months before my trip, but I never heard back from them. In the past, they have spoken very briefly with a small handful of journalists, but I was pretty sure they wouldn't want to speak to a stranger standing unannounced on their doorstep.

Their home didn't inspire me to try and talk to them then either. Set back from the road, the dark cream house with dusty blue shutters doesn't really look like anything special. Frankly, it was a little anticlimactic. Sure, it looked like a fine place to grow up, but it's not like we were driving by the Taj Mahal. And to be honest, I felt a little creepy and we sped away after only a minute of staring out the open car window.

Next up was the Chagrin Falls Library. Zo hooked us up with the staff and we were allowed to go downstairs and peruse the basement archives without supervision. I went hoping to find a cache of *Chagrin Valley Herald Sun* newspapers, first-hand looks at

Watterson's early editorial career. Though some of his *Cincinnati Post* and *Collegian* cartoons have made their way onto the web, this work has remained hidden away from curious cartoon historians.

The basement was warm and dark, a crude Petri dish for all the books that languish on row after row of gray metal shelving. We made our way into the far corner of the farthest room, where bound newspaper collections are haphazardly piled out of order. Despite the lack of organization, the 1977 book was near the top of the first stack I came across. There was a fine layer of dust on it and it clearly hadn't been cracked open any time this millennium, so the yellowed pages were in good condition.

I flipped through only a few issues and struck pay dirt. I guess those lucky rocket-ship underpants really do work! Watterson's style, even as a teenager, was unmistakable. Before I had even seen the signature, I knew it was his work. The characters were similar to those he had drawn in his college editorial cartoons during that same period. They had long legs, loose arms and purposely sloppy haircuts and wouldn't have looked out of place in *MAD* magazine. They were all clearly drawn by the same hand, but the artist behind that hand hadn't created something that was uniquely his yet.

The most eye-opening discovery I made was the pieces based around swimming-pool issues. Several of them include a bathing-suit-clad female who looks very much like a blonder, more curvaceous version of Rosalyn the babysitter, who was also Calvin's swimming instructor. There's one cartoon in particular wherein the Rosalyn-esque character is dipping her toe into the water and the similarity is striking, although Rosalyn would never show so much cleavage as her comic doppelgänger.

For the next hour, I flicked through hundreds of pages of old newsprint, relishing each new cartoon exhumation. This was a real bonanza and there were literally dozens of previously unseen works. Some made sense out of context, but many required some institutional knowledge of Chagrin Falls to even begin to make sense of, much less find them amusing. Unfortunately, most of them were in the former category and I knew I missed a lot of the inside jokes.

I made it all the way through 1979 before running out of both cartoons and time. After saying our goodbyes to Zo, we drove a couple of miles to the fringes of town to meet up with Watterson's old high-school buddy, David Bowe. He greeted us at the door and welcomed us into a cluttered living room that looked out over a backyard and a small pond where he fishes. Coincidentally, he had tried to call Watterson earlier that day, because he was going to see a production of *Stage Door* at the high school that night, the same play that Watterson starred in as a high-school senior. Bowe hadn't heard back from him and I detected an undercurrent of sadness from him over the course of our conversation, because it was apparent that the two friends don't talk as much or see each other as frequently as they once did.

Nonetheless, Bowe was happy to discuss his past with Watterson. As I made myself comfortable on the couch and set up my recorder, Bowe went into another room and brought back a couple of *Calvin and Hobbes* books. One was signed to him from Watterson and included a personal sketch of the doctor character. It's a one-off piece that would probably fetch thousands of dollars on eBay, but for Bowe it's a cherished reminder of their long-standing friendship. And though the character only appeared a handful of times, Bowe was clearly flattered by his inclusion. He was also saddened when the doctor didn't become a regularly occurring character. "I was hoping he'd do it more," Bowe admitted. "But Bill didn't want Calvin to appear as a kid who went to the doctor all the time."

Bowe pulled out a photo album and showed me a series of pictures of him, Watterson and their friends from high school and college. Most of the shots are just of the guys goofing off. A few show Watterson posing with his early artwork. As he showed us the photographs, it was clear that he still holds that time in his life close to his heart and he ended our conversation on a revealing, heartfelt note.

"It's been a great fortune of mine to grow up with Bill and watch this all happen," he said unguardedly. "There are hundreds of people who have grown up with somebody famous and were fairly close with them. It makes you realize that they're all just people. They seem like they're perfect, but they're not. Look at Britney Spears. She looks great, because they want her to look great, but if you met her in real life you probably wouldn't give her a second look. When you know someone like Bill, it puts life into perspective."

Bowe walked us out and we bid him goodbye from the cold of the driveway. As I looked back at him silhouetted in the doorway, his cartoon self became superimposed on his real form for a moment before the door shut. We drove out of town in the gathering darkness; Christmas lights flickered at us from front lawns and windows. By the time we made it to 71 South back to Mason, it was completely black out and the sides of the road dropped off into obsidian nothingness. The car was a little pod of luminosity zooming through this cloaked landscape and I felt like one of the miniature explorers in *The Fantastic Voyage*.

Over the course of two days, my subject had been transformed from this character I could only envision in my head into a tangible person. Seeing his work first hand, walking the streets where he grew up and talking to the people that knew him gave Watterson shape and form. He wasn't just a cartoonist; he was a friend, a local, a neighbor — somebody real. The trip brought him fully into focus and defined him as I had never seen him before.

CHAPTER 10

The Future is Always Uncertain

Coming back is really, really ill advised. I'm the expert at this. I returned with my eyes wide open to the fact that you can't go home again. Remember when Michael Jordan returned to basketball? That's all you need to know.

— Berke Breathed, creator of *Bloom County* and *Outland*

What kind of person would Calvin be if he had matured into his terrible teens? A sardonic rebel with a penchant for sci-fi novels, Tarantino movies and Norwegian death metal? The freaky kid that everyone is convinced is mad — or constantly stoned — because he still acts out one-sided fantasy sequences? A quasi-philosopher, mixing the insight of the Dalai Lama, Twain's moralism and Bill Hicks's philosophical humor? Who knows? I certainly don't.

But Calvin never progressed beyond his sixth birthday in the strip. So, even if he were still in newspapers, he'd still be up to his usual childish high jinks — throwing slush balls at Susie Derkins, getting sent to Mr Spittle's office and warring with the monsters under his bed. Which brings up the question on everyone's mind: Will Watterson's creations ever again ride a sled down a snowy hill or play a game of Calvinball? "It's my job to ask that question of him periodically, but I don't," Salem admitted to me during one of our last conversations. "I highly doubt it. I don't think he has that creative urge anymore. I think he felt like he said everything within that medium that he wanted to say or could say."

I asked West the same question and his response was also unpromising, mostly because he felt that Watterson wasn't temperamentally suited for the challenges of daily newspaper syndication. "It's funny, because his genius emerged due to the pressures that were placed upon him every day," West revealed to me. "*Calvin and Hobbes* would have not been created had it not been for that, because it required an extraordinary amount of discipline. Having newspaper editors and readers expecting to see you fill this hole is an extraordinary impetus for creation. And he rose to that challenge, but I don't think it came naturally to him. He didn't thrive on it and it took an extraordinary toll on him. Like the runner of a race, did he set the record? Yeah, he set the record. But does he want to do it again? Is it something he looks forward to? No, I don't think so."

Both men were equally doubtful that any further books will be forthcoming. "*The Complete Calvin and Hobbes* was a wonderful legacy to his achievements and we were delighted to be a part of it," Salem explained. "But I don't see anything beyond that." Although Watterson did produce several new pictures of his famous duo for that collection, in all likelihood, that will have been the last time he'd pick up the brush to draw a boy and his tiger.

As of this writing, no original *Calvin and Hobbes* strip has ever been put up for sale. If one did, conservative estimates place its value in the tens of thousands of dollars. I know more than a few people who would mortgage their house and send their offspring off to the salt mines for a few years to raise the funds necessary to own a piece of Watterson's legacy.

The news isn't all bad for those diehard fans who will follow Watterson wherever he goes artistically. West did admit that Watterson wasn't against the idea of exhibiting his recent paintings. "But it's very complicated," West told me. "If he does a gallery of landscapes, then why are people coming? If you put them up for sale, why are people buying them? The whole thing is now fraught with baggage that makes it uncomfortable to consider." He also believes that Watterson hasn't crafted enough work that he is proud enough to display. "It's not that he hasn't created many, many pieces of art," West clarified. "But that's different from, 'This is what I want to say to you.' I just don't think he has created a critical mass of art that he feels confident speaks to his current vision."

Avid Watterson fans might want to keep an eye on galleries in the Cleveland area, since he currently lives in an undisclosed location in one of its suburbs. He might use a small, local gallery to exhibit in — perhaps even under a pseudonym — to forgo the attention a large New York or Los Angeles show would bring. This way he would be able to get honest feedback on his work without jumping back into the maelstrom that he tried so hard to avoid the first time around.

The Cartoon Library & Museum still has its "Sunday Pages" exhibit in frames and could very well show it again or run a completely new show from their Watterson archives. Personally, I'd love to see an exhibit that celebrated the four seasons, which Watterson always drew with such beauty and vitality. And who knows? Maybe Watterson will reverse his position on all things *Calvin and Hobbes* related later in life for one reason or another. Anything is possible.

One project many have vainly wished for is an animated film. Ever since *Calvin and Hobbes* first came out, there has been an inordinate amount of interest in a movie, which has only grown in the absence of the strip. In 2005, rumors sprang up online that Watterson was finally working on a feature-length movie. This rumor was not immediately dismissible as an internet hoax because, in a 1989 interview with Richard West for *The Comics Journal*, Watterson had waffled on the possibility. "For all my admiration of the art, I really can't decide if I ever want to see *Calvin and Hobbes* animated," he admitted. "I know I'd enjoy working with the visual opportunities animation offers, but you change the world you've created when you change the medium in which it's presented . . . Another, more personal reservation I have is that animation, by necessity, is a team sport, and the fewer people with input into my work, the better I like it." Later in the same interview he relented somewhat by saying, "I'm reserving judgment on animation." While this was by no means a green light, it did leave the door open enough for fans to remain hopeful.

I asked Lee Salem if there were any possibility of its actually happening. "Sorry, no," he told me definitively. "At one point, we were trying to make one and he said to me, "I can't even imagine what the characters would sound like." And when you have that kind of creative issue, things don't go very far." In a related conversation with Rich West, he revealed to me that Watterson is a fan of animation genius and director Brad Bird, the man behind *Ratatouille* and *The Incredibles*. After some poking around the Pixar publicity department, I hunted down Bird at his home office to see what he would make of such a project.

It turns out there's a mutual admiration society in the making, because Bird is a big fan of Watterson. "*Calvin and Hobbes* had an animator's sensibility," Bird asserted at the beginning of our call. "One of the things they teach you in acting is that when you come on stage, the moment doesn't *begin* when you come on stage; you're coming from somewhere and you're coming from a series of experiences that have led to this moment. Not only in terms of your character's overall life, but on that particular day. What were you doing ten minutes before your entrance? What were you doing an hour before your entrance? It all has an effect on how you enter, so it's not a generic thing. The same goes for movement; you're coming from somewhere and you're going towards something. Watterson always found a great middle moment that always felt like the whole body was feeling the attitude. You can feel the moment before, and you can feel the moments that are coming after it. It feels like a piece of action rather than a pose."

When he wasn't admiring the movement and dynamism of the strip, Bird was enthralled with the Spaceman Spiff sequences. "Those scenes feel like movies," Bird said admiringly. "People oftentimes illustrate a kid's imagination with a kid's drawings, but the drawings are not the imagination. Watterson was really good about that, because the drawings were as real as reality. A kid's imagination of something that might be goofy or fantastic is vivid. Their ability to put it down on paper might be limited, but that's not their imagination. When Calvin would imagine something it was more like a really big budget movie."

If he were to make one of Calvin's imaginary big-budget movies, what would it look like? "Any true vision would have to be about Calvin's reality completely intruding on our own at will," Bird declared. "But the animation has to be done very, very well. Any version that I would either want to make or want to see would have to look absolutely like Bill Watterson's work. I would horsewhip animators for trying to redesign the characters in any way. They're perfect just the way they are." Bird does believe that there is a good version of the film floating out in the ether. "If the right choices were made and the right voices were done and the right animators came along, you could make something great," he told me. "Just look at what Peter Jackson did with the *Lord of the Rings* trilogy."

Bird then said that a film version has been on animators' wish lists as long as the strip has been around. Some animators he knows have even done pencil tests of the characters as school projects, though he hasn't. There are numerous instances of these short films on the web, though they are often taken down by vigilant YouTube censors. Unfortunately, none of these piratical clips comes close to getting it right. Having watched them a number of times myself, I guarantee that your search will probably end in disappointment. A flurry of questions such as, Did Calvin really sound like *that*?, Is that how Hobbes jumps?, and Why did they bother? run through your mind before you realize you shouldn't have bothered in the first place.

You can find more "bootleg" *Calvin and Hobbes* on other media platforms too. *The Boondocks*, *Garfield* and *Zits*, as well as many other comic strips, have all alluded to the strip, while *MAD* magazine ran a parody 'toon called *Calvin and Jobs* and *Family Guy* had a brief appearance from Calvin and Hobbes in 2009. Perhaps the most disturbing use of Calvin and Hobbes was on Seth Green's *Robot Chicken*, which did a stop-motion segment in which the parents think Calvin has gone insane, because he imagines his stuffed animal is alive. Calvin is sent to a shrink and given electroshock therapy before being sent home, where he slaughters his parents for not believing him. The short clip ends with Calvin in a straightjacket locked up in a padded room talking to a stuffed tiger. Thanks, but I think I'll let my future kids watch *Finding Nemo* instead.

Though these reminders of *Calvin and Hobbes* are out there, it's not the same as having the original. Newspapers are emptier without Watterson's daily injection of humor and philosophy. Some days, when the front page was covered in nothing but bad news, *Calvin and Hobbes* was the one bright spot in the entire paper. I have sympathy for people who don't have that moment of childish joy to look forward to every day and hope they can still find it in *Pearls Before Swine, Cul de Sac* or their daily horoscope. There's always the books to reread, but that's about it. There's nothing more out there.

But what kind of ending is that? You may ask, and rightfully so. I asked myself the same question when I arrived at this point in my storytelling. With two months to go before my deadline, I didn't have an ending befitting a journey of this magnitude. A more satisfying cap to this whole expedition was needed. Sure, I had told myself that I was going to approach this project as if Watterson had joined the choir invisible, but since there was no actual death, I was at a loss.

It had been months since I had written my letter to Watterson, but I hadn't heard a peep. Not even a "No thanks," a "Go screw yourself," or a "I didn't talk to Spielberg, why would I talk to you?" Each week that went by without a response made me more and more despondent. It reminded me of when I was six and a day could feel like a week, a week like a month, and a month itself was far too long an amount of time to even try to comprehend.

Not willing to go down without a fight, I made one last appeal to Watterson, with the "Hail Mary" hope that he might decide to stop channeling Salinger for a brief moment. I still didn't want to call, because I was sure that would be totally catastrophic. I didn't want the two things I heard from Watterson to be an F-bomb and the click of the phone hanging up. Sending another letter struck me as repetitive and doomed to failure, so I brought up my quandary with Lee Salem, who had been so helpful over the course of the project. Perhaps out of sheer pity, he generously offered to ask Bill in person about participating in the book when he visited the cartoonist in a few weeks' time.

I was buoyed by Salem's offer, but worried that if it didn't happen, I would be up against my deadline with nowhere to turn and even less time to salvage my ending. But what else was I going to do, aside from offering up my prayers to any and all deities? Buddha, Virgin de Guadalupe, Gandalf and good old-fashioned God all got entreaties. I even carried around a lucky penny for a week hoping to tip the scales of fate in my direction.

When I finally heard back from Salem a few weeks later, I took the call with equal amounts of anticipation and trepidation (and a lucky penny in my right pocket). Like all trips to the firing squad, the bad news came quickly. "He said, "Why is he doing this? Who cares?"" Salem related to me. Coming from a guy like Watterson who studied art history, this struck me then and does now as more than a little obtuse. "You're a famous artist who has influenced thousands of people and made millions more laugh," I wanted to scream in frustration in the general direction of Cleveland. "Of course people want to know about you!" But instead, I bit my tongue and thanked Lee again for all his help over the course of this project.

As my wife will tell you, I can be a pessimistic person. However, I'm also an unabashedly hopeful guy and after all, wasn't 2008 the year that hope won? When I began researching and writing this book, I knew I was facing impossible odds — much like a drunken 80-year-old trying to scale Mount Everest in a leisure suit and flip-flops. My phone call with Lee went exactly as I had expected it to, but I still couldn't help feeling a momentary pang of disappointment.

But disappointment doesn't meet deadlines, so I threw myself back into the wordy fray. Early mornings and late nights were the routine, with lots of caffeine in between. I still hadn't decided what I was going to do, but I had this weird feeling that something would happen. I'm a big believer in karma and I'd thrown a supertanker full of the stuff at this project, so didn't the Universe owe me?

Whether it was karma or just sheer luck, I got a response from the great beyond a couple of weeks before my deadline. Zo, my tour guide in Chagrin Falls, had run into Bill's mother, Kathryn Watterson, on the street. Taking my future in her hands, Zo made an impromptu pitch on the spot: Would Kathryn agree to talk to me?

Mrs Watterson was hesitant. She was unsure if she would be comfortable discussing her son and whether she could be of any help. But she nonetheless gave Zo her home phone number and agreed to at least talk to me, though she wouldn't definitively commit to an interview. When I got this juicy tidbit in my inbox late one Thursday night, I let out a whoop and did a little dance (I'm not ashamed — no one was there to video me). This was it! The best finale I could hope for.

A few days later, I telephoned Kathryn Watterson with more than a little nervous acid churning a hole in my stomach. "I was wondering when you would call," she said when I introduced myself. "I've heard a lot about this project." She was sitting in the living room of the house Bill grew up in, surrounded by reminders of her son. There are several *Calvin and Hobbes* strips hanging up near where she is sitting that draw on parental inspiration. In one, Calvin's father is insisting he eat his meal (a "disgusting slimy blob," according to Calvin), because it has the potential to build character. In another, Calvin calls his dad at the patent office and insists he tell him a story.

Mrs Watterson was warm and unflustered by my call, but I didn't know how long she would stay on the phone, so I plunged right in (after quadruple-checking that my digital recorder was actually recording). I explained the scope of my project and recounted how many cartoonists and artists I'd spoken with who had been greatly influenced by her son, which seemed to please her. After my pitch was on the table, I delicately asked if she wouldn't mind answering some questions. If she felt as though I crossed any boundaries, she was happy to tell me so and I would try to ensure that my questions didn't impose upon her private relationship with her son. Over the course of our conversation, she balked only once, but was otherwise as open as her loyalties would allow. It is the longest interview she — or anyone in her family — has ever given about Bill. It's also the culmination of two years' worth of phone calls, emails, letters and prostrations to the void.

I asked at the outset whether people still contact her to ask about her son or show up on their doorstep looking for autographs. "Not any more," she admitted. "Most people are friendly and just want to say, "I like his work." This country has such an odd attachment to people in the limelight and that's another reason that Bill does not want to be in the limelight. Besides he doesn't appreciate that at all.

I've heard him say, "I haven't done anything that advances the world in any way, shape, or form except maybe made them smile once in a while. So why are they after me?" and I'm sure he'd ask you "Why are you writing a book about me? I'm a dull person, just living my life."" I replied that when she told him about this project, she should tell him that I just wanted to know more about the journey he took that crossed ten years' worth of cartoon panels.

Though they have come to accept his success, she and her husband certainly had no idea that their son was going to grow into a cartoonist of such renown. They did realize his proclivity for art at an early age: "The kid was born with a pencil," she told me with a laugh. "Not that we ever really thought he would be able to make a living at cartooning. That's not because we didn't have faith in our son; it's just that it is an extremely hard thing to get into. When he got the job in Cincinnati, I thought he could be a political cartoonist, but then he lost that job very quickly. But to be a strip cartoonist? I thought that could never happen. I never did worry about him, because I thought this is what people do: you have a dream and if you can realize it, fine. But if you can't, you adjust." Their other son, Tom, had dreams of being a rock star. That didn't work out. He became a teacher and she thinks that worked out for the best.

She didn't see her son in Calvin ("He had a much more vivid mind than he ever had actions") and she never saw herself as Calvin's mother. "I see the mom as sort of being generic mom," Kathryn admitted. "But I see my husband a lot. I'm thinking of references to running, eating oatmeal and the green food. We're careful of our diet and we did a lot of running in our day. We were always trying to get the kids to eat well." Calvin's parents often extolled many of the same values she and her husband espoused. "I think they're typical values of a lot of families of the '60s and '70s," she reasoned. "Not watching TV, the babysitter and not going out very often — that's how we lived in small town Ohio."

She revealed that Bill had also drawn on personal experience when writing about Calvin's family's summer camping trips. The Wattersons went to a small island in Canada for camping trips a few times. "My husband was enthusiastic about those trips; the rest of us just went along for the ride," Kathryn told me with a good-natured chuckle. "It was really primitive sometimes. I remember the camp, the tent, the rain and brushing my teeth in the lake." She added, "I don't wash my hair in a lake anymore."

These trips down memory lane made opening the paper every day a beloved ritual. "It was almost like getting a letter or a call from Bill," Mrs Watterson told me. "We would recognize things from our lives, things that he believed in or funny things from the neighborhood. It was just wonderful."

Though she has a difficult time picking out her favorite strips, she was drawn to the environmentally conscious strips and the series about the dead raccoon. "Bill had a little raccoon that he found in the yard," she remembered to me. "He took care of and it died; that actually happened." Considering Watterson had written that this raccoon storyline had been inspired by a dead kitten his wife had found, this is of particular interest. "I remember the raccoon's death was a sad thing," Kathryn continued. "I remember Calvin's reaction: "I had to say good-bye as soon as I said hello." It was his first time seeing death. I thought that the depiction of how a child sees death and the child's reaction was done well. It wasn't the sort of thing you expect to find in the comics section."

Though she has many fond memories of the strip, her memories of her son's battle with the syndicate are darker. "It seemed like a great idea: to have your standards and not sell out if you didn't want to," she reasoned. "But it isn't really selling out here; it's the "American Way" in a lot of ways. I was proud that Bill chose his own path and never wavered from it." This was the extent to which she would talk about this part of her son's life.

She had a motherly, pragmatic approach to her son's decision to end the strip. "I was sad because I enjoyed it so much," she admitted. "But I knew he was ready to go on. You want your children to be happy and to be satisfied with their lives. So if that's what he needed to do, then that was fine."

"When you have children, you want them to realize something they've dreamed of," she told me at the end of our conversation. "That definitely happened to him. And it's interesting to see that even though it was his dream, he consciously rejected it after ten years and went on to a different kind of life. That's interesting and exciting to see. [Novelist F. Scott] Fitzgerald says, "There're no second acts in American lives," but I don't think that's necessarily true."

We said our goodbyes and I thanked her for spending time talking with me. This was my ending! I found it! Sweet victory was mine! Praise to the god of plenty!

After calming down, I returned to her last comment. I couldn't agree more with it; Fitzgerald truly missed the boat on that one. America absolutely loves somebody who confounds us with their second act. Just think of Paul Newman (actor-turned-humanitarian) and Ronald Reagan (actor-turned-president). We love it, because in the face of overwhelming odds these people achieved the great American dream not once, but twice. The funny thing about

Watterson is that he achieved that dream once, realized it wasn't what he was looking for and retreated to enjoy a far simpler dream.

Watterson's mother sounded truly pleased that her son had a second act as a family man. He found joy twice in his life and on his own terms in each instance. Her happiness confirmed something that I had suspected all along: Bill took great pleasure from the simple act of cartooning. Everything else that came from it — the money, the recognition, the licensing offers — all of that was just static to him, interfering with the harmony of creating. When you derive such happiness from something in your life, it's incredibly difficult to watch that thing become corrupted, because it makes you resent that which you love so much.

Many people don't do what they love for a living, so it's only natural for them to dislike their jobs. A lot of people approach work as something they expect to dislike, because that's what we're taught. TGIF, Hump Day happy hour, weekend warriors and all that other "work sucks" propaganda. Despite this, there are millions of people out there who absolutely love their jobs. They are defined by their work, they give it their everything and they can't imagine doing anything else. The one time I went skydiving, my instructor told me something simply profound somewhere around 20,000 feet: "If you love what you do, you never have to go to work a day in your life." Then we rolled forward out of the plane and into the nothingness. I didn't have time to think about it much then, because I was too busy screaming and wondering if the 'chute would open, but later, after a few bracing G&Ts, it made perfect sense.

Watterson was one of those guys that had to cartoon, because that's who he was. Even when he wasn't getting paid to do it, he had to do it. And when cartooning wasn't something he could love anymore, he had to stop doing it. He was always following his passion. Maybe that's why he doesn't understand why people would be interested in his life, because he was just doing what came naturally to him. Perhaps for him, my approaching him to be a part of this book was like a fan going up to Leonard Cohen when he was soul searching at the Zen Buddhist monastery and asking him to sing "Hallelujah" after morning meditation.

No matter what he does in the future, Watterson will always do what he wants to do. He's an iconoclast who would hate being called an iconoclast, a classic American artist who has forever elevated the world of cartooning to somewhere new and more special. What he left behind will always ring true to those lucky enough to discover and explore it.

Epilogue

> The great thing about American vernacular expression — whether it's rock 'n' roll, comic books or comic strips — is the way it becomes permission for some artists to do something so personal and so complete. The fact that it seems to be a disposable context invites some to be half-assed, but Watterson found the will to make something singular and beautiful.
>
> — Jonathan Lethem, author of *The Fortress of Solitude*

I began writing this book with a profound love and respect for Watterson and his work. Along the way, he frustrated me as a subject and often left me quietly (and, occasionally, very loudly) fuming. Not because he wouldn't cooperate with me — though I can't deny that my ego did feel mildly bruised by his rejection — but because he was such an enigma and I wanted to break the code. I've always loved piecing together puzzles, but I learned at an early age that it's no fun to do a puzzle when some of its pieces are missing, because it'll never be finished.

I had an epiphany near the end of writing this book, which made me realize that I was in the midst of an archeologist's puzzle, something wholly different from your usual look-at-the-box-and-make-the-pretty-picture type of puzzle. The archeologist accepts at the outset that all the pieces aren't there and they don't even know what they're trying to put together. But that's the challenge and the process of discovery. Like a dinosaur skeleton I discovered in a back-yard dig, I had uncovered something new and wondrous. All these new bits and pieces I'd learned about Watterson were fragments to a story that had never been told.

I laid out the pieces I had uncovered on the floor of my study and stepped back to see what I might imagine. There were *Calvin and Hobbes* collections, books, magazines, newspapers, birth certificates, letters, comic books, Post-it notes, receipts, cartoons, notebooks, and a dictionary all swirled together, plus a litany of half-drunk bottles of sparkling water and dirty plates. As I dug for information, I would move these mountains of ephemera around, hoping to find the sense within it all. Some days I'd be struck with insight and on others I would just stare blankly at it all, a simian idiot.

It's odd to think of a life in terms of a pile of lifeless organic matter. I suppose that's what I'll be when my ashes are scattered and I become a citizen of the great beyond. I am just practicing for the inevitable. The new piece of pulp that came out of that paper mael-strom — what you hold in your hands — was born out of a very personal journey. *Looking for Calvin and Hobbes* took me all across America — from Washington, DC, to Los Angeles and from Ohio to Indiana. It was accomplished late at night, early in the morning and on the weekends, in between doing my job, planning a wedding and indulging in the art of baking. It was not always easy and it came close to driving me into short-term insanity on a number of occasions.

I didn't really know what I was getting into when I first set out to write this book. Each little tidbit that came to light along the way felt like a minor revelation as I stitched together the life story of a private, talented man, a man who gave so much and didn't want very much in return. At moments I was confounded and frustrated by his utter lack of willingness to publicly engage his audience. In others, I found myself rooting for him as he stood up to what must have been overwhelming pressure.

The entire time I wrote, I kept returning to Watterson's work. *Calvin and Hobbes* was what set me down the path to this book, and what kept me on it when I was feeling lost or discouraged. I have one strip hanging over my desk that gets more appropriate as the last few days before my deadline tick away. Calvin is playing in the sandbox as Hobbes walks up and asks him if he has an idea for the story he's supposed to write for his homework assignment. "You can't just turn on creativity like a faucet. You have to be in the right mood," Calvin protests. Hobbes asks him what mood that is. "Last minute panic," Calvin replies calmly, as he keeps pushing his toy cars through the sand.

At the end of any of my projects I always feel a mixture of relief, joy, doubt and, yes, last-minute panic. My work was about to move out of my hands and into the larger world where you will judge, love, hate or ignore it. For ten years Watterson did that almost every day, and at a huge personal cost. When I look back at this story of a man, a boy and his tiger, I don't think about the pain and the darkness that lurked at the edges of this story. Instead, I think of all those mornings when I woke up from one dream only to plunge into another. *Calvin and Hobbes* reminded me daily that imagination is the element that elevates life from the mundane to the unforgettable. Thanks, Bill, our lives are richer for that reminder.

I'm going to go now; I have some exploring to do.

Some Random Tidbits You Might Like To Know But Which Didn't Make the Book

David Spade has a tattoo of Calvin.

Calvin wishes the Big Bang was called the "horrendous space kablooie" and the tyrannosaur the "monstrous killer death lizard."

The American Political Tradition and the Men Who Made It begins, "Long ago Horace White observed that the Constitution of the United States "is based upon the philosophy of Hobbes and the religion of Calvin. It assumes that the natural state of mankind is a state of war, and that the carnal mind is at enmity with God.""

Watterson loved the Beatles, and John Lennon once said, "Reality leaves a lot to the imagination."

Calvin is under the misimpression that BC stands for Before Calvin.

There is a website dedicated to all the stickers that show Calvin urinating on stuff. If you don't believe me, you can see for yourself at: http://www.annoying.com/nightmares/obsessive/02/0001/gallery.html

Environmentally friendly cleaner Citra-Solv recently came with a mini-comic called *Rustle The Leaf*, which proudly boasted that it was called the ""Green" *Calvin and Hobbes*."

In 2008, a group of Washington University students organized a live Calvinball game. One of the organizers boasted, "We strive for a certain level of confusion."

After *Jurassic Park* came out, Watterson refrained from putting dinosaurs in his strips for six months.

When I typed the phrase "Calvin and Hobbes are amazing" into Google, it came back with over 149,000 results.

Calvin's favorite books are by Mabel Syrup: *Hamster Huey and the Gooey Kablooie*; and its sequel, *Commander Coriander Salamander and 'er Singlehander Bellylander*.

I love cupcakes and I'm hungry. Mmmm . . . cupcakes.

SELECTED BIBLIOGRAPHY

Amend, Bill. Email interview by Nevin Martell. 23 July 2008.

—— (1989), *FoxTrot*. Foreword by Bill Watterson. Kansas City: Andrews and McMeel Publishing.

Anderson, Brad. Phone interview with Nevin Martell. 18 August 2008.

Andrews and McMeel Publishing (2005), "Press Release . . . *The Complete Calvin and Hobbes*: fans from around the world interview Bill Watterson." http://www.andrewsmcmeel.com/calvinandhobbes/interview.html

Astor, David (1986), "An overnight success after five years: cartoonist Bill Watterson struggled with several comics during the early 1980s before hitting it big with *Calvin and Hobbes*." *Editor & Publisher*, 8 February 1986: 34.

—— (1987), "A surprising Reuben for Bill Watterson." *Editor & Publisher*, 30 May 1987: 54.

—— (1989), "*Calvin and Hobbes* creator wins again." *Editor & Publisher*, 27 May 1989: 78.

—— (1992), "More response to half-page *Calvin* strip: the AASFE protests Sunday size requirement in letter to Universal, and a syndicate executive and cartoonist offer their opinions." *Editor & Publisher*, 11 January 1992: 30.

—— (1994), "The latest on *Calvin and Hobbes*." *Editor & Publisher*, 19 March 1994: 59.

Barry, Dave. Phone interview with Nevin Martell. 15 September 2008.

Bernstein, Adam (1997), "Calvin's unauthorized leak: stock car fans misuse comics character." *Washington Post*, 17 July 1997: B9.

Bird, Brad. Phone interview with Nevin Martell. 26 August 2008.

Borgman, Jim, with an introduction by Bill Watterson (1995), *Disturbing the Peace*. Cincinnati: Colloquial Books.

—— Email interview with Nevin Martell. 20 June 2008.

Bowe, David. In-person interview with Nevin Martell. 22 November 2008.

Boynton, Sandy. Email interview with Nevin Martell. 14 August 2008.

Breathed, Berke. Email interview with Nevin Martell. 11 June 2008.

—— Phone interview with Nevin Martell. 17 June 2008.

—— (2004), *OPUS: 25 Years of His Sunday Best*. New York: Little, Brown and Company.

Buford, Brendan. Phone interview with Nevin Martell. 5 September 2008.

Carroll, Jerry (1995), "*Calvin and Hobbes* to end." *San Francisco Chronicle*, 30 December 1995: C1.

Caswell, Lucy. In-person interview with Nevin Martell. 21 November 2008.

Cavna, Michael (2008), "Interview with the artist: *Cul de Sac*'s Richard Thompson." *Comic Riffs* blog on http://www.washingtonpost.com, 18 August.

Christian, Barbara (1996), "Window on Main Street: famous cartoonist buys house back in hometown." *Chagrin Valley Times*, 25 January 1996: B3.

Christie, Andrew (1987), "Bill Watterson interview." *Honk!*, no. 2, January 1987: 28–33.

Coverly, Dave. Phone interview with Nevin Martell. 25 August 2008.

Darcy, Jeff. Phone interview with Nevin Martell. 9 July 2008.

Davis, Jim. Email interview with Nevin Martell. 8 July 2008.

Dean, Paul (1987), "*Calvin and Hobbes* creator draws on the simple life." *Los Angeles Times*, 1 April 1987.

Duke, Sara. Phone interview with Nevin Martell. 16 April 2008.

Eliot, Jan. Phone interview with Nevin Martell. 19 August 2008.

Ellers, Richard (1986), "Calvin has cartoonist by the tail." *Cleveland Plain Dealer*, 5 October 1986: 21-A.

—— Phone interview with Nevin Martell. 21 October 2008.

Farago, Andrew. Phone interview with Nevin Martell. 4 June 2008.

Foley, Bill. Phone interview with Nevin Martell. 4 December 2008.

Garhart, Martin. Phone interview with Nevin Martell. 5 February 2009.

Gillespie, Sarah. Phone interview with Nevin Martell. 12 August 2008.

Groth, Gary (1997), "Schulz at 3 o'clock in the morning." *The Comics Journal*, no. 200, December 1997: 27.

Gurewitch, Nicholas. Phone interview with Nevin Martell. 3 July 2008.

Harvey, Robert C. (1994), *The Art of the Funnies: An Aesthetic History*. Jackson: University Press of Mississippi.

Hendin, Dave. Phone interview with Nevin Martell. 16 September 2008.

Herriman, George, with a foreword by Bill Watterson (1990), *The Komplete Kolor Krazy Kat*. Princeton: Kitchen Sink Press.

"In search of Bill Watterson." *Jawbone with Len Nora* podcast from http://jawboneradio.blogspot.com/2005/11/jawbone-81-in-search-of-bill-watterson.html, 2 November 2005.

Jantze, Michael. Phone interviews with Nevin Martell. 5 and 8 August 2008.

Johnston, Lynn. Phone interview with Nevin Martell. 15 August 2008.

Keefe, Mike. Phone interview with Nevin Martell. 2 May 2008.

Knight, Keith. Phone interview with Nevin Martell. 14 August 2008.

Kohn, Martin F. (1987), "Drawing the (comic) line: *Calvin and Hobbes* artist struggled before attaining success." *Houston Chronicle*, 26 April 1987: ZEST section, p. 11.

Kuehner, John C. (1998), "*Calvin* creator's secret hideout: cartoonist Bill Watterson returns to a cloistered life." *Cleveland Plain Dealer*, 20 December 1998.

Lethem, Jonathan. Phone interview with Nevin Martell. 15 July 2008.

McCay, Winsor, with an essay by Bill Watterson (1997), *The Best of Little Nemo in Slumberland*. New York: Stewart, Tabori & Chang.

Mallett, Jef. Phone interview with Nevin Martell. 26 August 2008.

Meddick, Jim. Phone interview with Nevin Martell. 19 August 2008.

Nordling, Lee (1995), *Your Career In Comics*. Kansas City: Andrews and McMeel Publishing.

"Notice to comics readers." *Washington Post*, 29 December 1995.

Oliphant, Patrick. Phone interview with Nevin Martell. 13 August 2008.

Oswalt, Patton. Phone interview with Nevin Martell. 1 June 2008.

Parisi, Mark. Phone interview with Nevin Martell. 1 July 2008.

Pastis, Stephan. Phone interview with Nevin Martell. 10 July 2008.

Peters, Mike. Phone interview with Nevin Martell. 10 September 2008.

Price, Hilary. Phone interview with Nevin Martell. 7 August 2008.

Reagan, Michael. Phone interview with Nevin Martell. 17 November 2008.

Renner, James (2003), "Missing!: *Calvin and Hobbes* creator Bill Watterson. Last seen in northeast Ohio. Do not approach." *Cleveland Scene*, 26 November 2003.

Rhode, Michael G. (1999), "The commercialization of comics: a broad historical overview." *International Journal of Comic Art*, 1: 2, Fall 1999.

Robb, Jenny. In-person interview with Nevin Martell. 11 December 2008.

Rubin, Robert A. (1980), "Watterson ends collegian reign, heads for Cincinnati." *Kenyon Collegian*, 1 May 1980: 6.

Salem, Lee. Phone interviews with Nevin Martell. 18 April 2008 and 3 October 2008.

Schulz, Jeannie. Email interview with Nevin Martell. 12 July 2008.

Smith, Jeff. Phone interview with Nevin Martell. 21 October 2008.

"So Long, Charlie Brown." *The News Hour with Jim Lehrer*. PBS, 3 January 2000.

Sullivan, Timy (1978), "*Herald* cartoonist says it ain't easy." *Chagrin Valley Herald Sun*, 12 January 1978: A1 and B5.

Tatulli, Mark. Phone interview with Nevin Martell. 16 May 2008.

Tenney, Tom. Phone interview with Nevin Martell. 4 August 2008.

Thompson, Craig. Phone interview with Nevin Martell. 9 July 2008.

Thompson, Richard. In-person interview with Nevin Martell. 6 April 2008.

Thompson, Richard, with a foreword by Bill Watterson (2008), *Cul de Sac: This Exit*. Kansas City: Andrews and McMeel.

Troop, Steve. Phone interview with Nevin Martell. 25 August 2008.

Tucker, Neely (2005), "The tiger strikes again: after an early bedtime, Calvin and Hobbes are up and running in a new collection." *Washington Post*, 4 October 2005: C1.

Universal Press Syndicate sales and promotional materials. 1987, 1991.

Walker, Brian. Phone interview with Nevin Martell. 1 June 2008.

Walker, Mort. Phone interview with Nevin Martell. 2 December 2008.

"*Wall Street Journal* somehow tracks down Bill Watterson." *New York* magazine online. http://nymag.com/daily/entertainment/2007/10/wall_street_journal_somehow_fi.html, 15 October 2007.

Washington, Julie (1986), "Cartoon caprices: artist finally draws a winner." *Cleveland Plain Dealer*, 1 March 1986: 1-B and 6-B.

Watterson, Bill (1985), "Book review: *The Great Communicator.*" *Target*, no. 18, Winter 1985–6.

—— (1987), *Calvin and Hobbes*. Kansas City: Andrews and McMeel.

—— (1988), *Something Under the Bed Is Drooling: A Calvin and Hobbes Collection*. Kansas City: Andrews and McMeel.

—— (1988), *The Essential Calvin and Hobbes: A Calvin and Hobbes Treasury*. Kansas City: Andrews and McMeel.

—— (1989), "The cheapening of the comics." Speech given at the Festival of Cartoon Art, Ohio State University, 27 October 1989.

—— (1989), *The Calvin & Hobbes Lazy Sunday Book*. Kansas City: Andrews and McMeel.

—— (1989), *Yukon Ho!*. Kansas City: Andrews and McMeel.

—— (1990), "Some thoughts on the real world by one who glimpsed it and fled." Commencement speech given at Kenyon College, 20 May 1990.

—— (1990), *The Authoritative Calvin and Hobbes*. Kansas City: Andrews and McMeel.

—— (1990), *Weirdos from Another Planet!*. Kansas City: Andrews and McMeel.

—— (1991), *Scientific Progress Goes "Boink."* Kansas City: Andrews and McMeel.

—— (1991), *The Revenge of the Baby-Sat*. Kansas City: Andrews and McMeel.

—— (1992), *Attack of the Deranged Mutant Killer Monster Snow Goons*. Kansas City: Andrews and McMeel.

—— (1992), *The Indispensable Calvin and Hobbes*. Kansas City: Andrews and McMeel.

—— (1993), *The Days Are Just Packed*. Kansas City: Andrews and McMeel.

—— (1994), *Homicidal Psycho Jungle Cat*. Kansas City: Andrews and McMeel.

—— (1995), *The Calvin and Hobbes Tenth Anniversary Book*. Kansas City: Andrews and McMeel.

—— (1996), *It's a Magical World*. Kansas City: Andrews and McMeel.

—— (1996), *There's Treasure Everywhere: A Calvin and Hobbes Collection*. Kansas City: Andrews and McMeel.

—— (1998), "Some thoughts on *Pogo* & comic strips today." *Cartoonist PROfiles*, no. 80, December 1988: 12–19.

—— (1999), "Drawn into a dark but gentle world." *Los Angeles Times*, 21 December 1999.

—— (2001), *Calvin and Hobbes: Sunday Papers, 1985–1995*. Kansas City: Andrews and McMeel.

—— (2005), *The Complete Calvin and Hobbes*. Kansas City: Andrews and McMeel.

—— (2007), "The grief that made *Peanuts* good." *Wall Street Journal*, 12 October 2007.

"Watterson, Fuhry nominees in national essay contest." *Valley Lantern*, 17 April 1975: 6.

Watterson, Kathryn. Phone interview with Nevin Martell. 28 January 2009.

West, Rich (1989), "Interview: Bill Watterson." *The Comics Journal*, no. 127, March: 56–71.

West, Rich. Phone interviews with Nevin Martell. 10 June 2008 and 17 July 2008.

Williams, Gene (1987), "Watterson: Calvin's other alter ego." *Cleveland Plain Dealer*, 30 August 1987.

ACKNOWLEDGMENTS

This book has consumed the last year of my life. Subsequently, I owe more than a few people my endless thanks, as well as a few apologies.

This book would not have been possible without the dedicated and detailed work of my research assistants. Mark Soto helped me get the ball rolling, for which I'm very grateful. Matt Zdancewicz and Sara Tenenbaum toiled long hours for no more compensation than a few free meals and my eternal gratitude. And Savannah Guernsey was the wind that carried me over the finish line when I needed it most. Thanks to all of you for rocking the casbah.

My warmest gratitude to my editor, David Barker, who helped transform a zygote of an idea into this endearing love child of a book. Katie Gallof at Continuum gets her own appreciative backslap for all her help, too.

Many, many appreciations go out to everyone who agreed to be interviewed for this project or helped me out along the way: Brian Walker, Patton Oswalt, Richard Thompson, Sara W. Duke, Tim Hulsizer, Mike Keefe, Tom Tenney, Mike Rhode, Mark Tatulli, Andrew Farago and Summerlea Kashar at the Cartoon Art Museum, Phil Nel, Jim Borgman, Mark Parisi, Nicholas Gurewitch, Harvey

Pekar (thanks for the call, Harvey; you made my day), Jonathan Lethem, Jeannie Schulz, Stephan Pastis, Jeff Darcy, Sam Douglas, Hilary Price, Ron Goulart, Laura Jordan, Lynn Johnston, Sandy Boynton, Matt Tauber, Jim Davis, Kim Campbell, Keith Knight, Paige Braddock, Sarah Gillespie, Jennifer Collet, Jim Meddick, Brad Anderson, Steve Argula and Amy Ellenwood at Pixar, Brad Bird, Dave Coverly, Steve Troop, Jef Mallett, Gene Weingarten, Mike Peters, Dave Hendin, Dave Barry, Brendan Burford, Bill Foley, Jan Eliot, David Sedaris (your postcard was a really uplifting moment; thank you), Robin McCarthy, Richard Ellers, Michael Reagan, Martin Garhart, Joseph Slate, Philip Hooker, Mort Walker, Jeff Smith, Patrick Oliphant, Craig Thompson and Bill Amend.

Lucy Caswell, Jenny Robb and Susan Liberator at the Ohio State Cartoon Library & Museum — my appreciations go out to you for your tremendous help with the researching of this book.

Many thanks to everyone in Chagrin Falls who helped make this book a great joy to research — Pat Zalba at the Chagrin Falls Historical Society, Tom Mattern, Dr David Bowe, Phil at Fireside Books and Claude at the library. An exceptional thanks is due to Zo Sykora — a wonderful tour guide and a kick-ass co-conspirator.

Special thanks are reserved for Lee Salem, Rich West and Kathryn Watterson. I appreciate you all opening up and trusting me with your stories.

More special thanks to Berke Breathed and Michael Jantze for ushering me into the wide, wonderful and, frankly, twisted world of cartooning. You both aided me immensely and this book would not have been the same without your help and humor.

Every one of my projects has a soundtrack that got me through the tough parts and helped me celebrate the joyous moments.

This time it was Kings of Leon's *Only By The Night*, Fleet Foxes' eponymous LP, Animal Collective's *Strawberry Jam* and British Sea Power's *Do You Like Rock Music?* My gratitude goes out to all the fine gents behind these inspirational albums.

Everyone at Story House Productions deserves a thank you for putting up with me on a daily basis, especially the development team: Andreas, Carsten, Drew, Laurie and Jess. An additional "hollah" goes to my corner posse — Ben, Stephon and Julia — who are constantly assaulted by my cranked-up iTunes and my mouth on the babble setting.

A big, collective hug goes to the friends who make my life a wonderful, high jinks-fueled journey: Jeb Gray, James Steerman, Shelby and Vaj, Matt Soltysiak, Weijia Jiang, Dan and Laura, the Hurs, the entire Liss family (there are too many of you now!), the Zartarians, the Abodeelys, Michael Krugman (the godfather of my career), Shawna Friedman and family, the Clinton crew (Brendon, Eli, Ke), Sue Waldman, Neil Nathan, Mark "Growch" Growchoski, Derek Monteverdi, and anyone else I forgot in the haste to finish this section. Mad props to Danny Fowler for making me better than I deserve.

Tomer, Sam, Rya and Talia Avivi deserve a singular "adank" for putting me up in Ohio and coming along on my wild ride into the heart of cartooning history.

My roommates, Sam Abdelhamid and Pritham Khalsa, receive extra hugs, high fives and cupcakes for their long-standing support and willingness to talk to me, even when I was so fried I didn't make much sense.

The Labor Day posse — Ravi Davis, Josh Nicotra and Mike Keenan — get a special shout out, as do their long-suffering wives and children, Dana, Brandy, Phin and Eowyn.

I often say that I am blessed with a wonderful family, but that barely scratches the surface. Mum, thanks for always being a warm heart, a bright soul and an open mind. Dad, endless gratitude for always supporting me and reminding me that it is oftentimes the simple pleasures in life that are the most rewarding. Josephine, I couldn't have asked for a better sibling — you know when to make me laugh, when to listen and when to spring into action. Will, I don't know how you maintain your stoicism and good humor in the face of such constant mayhem; you have my respect for that alone. And dearest Flossie, you are a shining star; I love you endlessly. Maribeth and Paul Mullen, I'm still just getting to know you, but I look forward to deepening that relationship in the years to come. To the Murrays (and Spiegels), much love to you all. Hurrah hurrah for our fabulous family and all our quirky, charming traditions — the curd, Boxing Day, walking the Horn, sailing on *Serendipity*, Gentlemen's Adventures and don't forget the shoofly pie! And to my Ghanaian family — Mr and Mrs O, Yom and Yao — I love being a part of your lives and getting to know you all better. Thanks for always making Kwame feel at home.

Last, but never least, I want to thank my beautiful, caring and eternally patient wife, Indira. I used the advance from this book to buy your engagement ring, so I wanted it to be nothing short of amazing, just like you. I hope it lives up to that high standard you set. Much love and kind appreciations for all your encouragement, edits and empanadas. You are the world to me.

Cover yourself in black gold dust
Lie back in the sound
For one moment we're untouchable
Nothing can bring us down

— Bravado

INDEX